On Friendship

THEMES FOR THE 21ST CENTURY

Titles in this series

On Friendship

RAY PAHL

Polity

First published in 2000 by Polity Press in association with Blackwell
Publishers Ltd

Reprinted 2006

Polity Press
65 Bridge Street
Cambridge CB2 1UR, UK

Polity Press
350 Main Street
Malden, MA 02148, USA

Library of Congress Cataloging-in-Publication Data
Pahl, R. E. (Raymond Edward), 1935-
  On friendship / Ray Pahl.
    p.cm.—(Themes for the 21st century)
  Includes bibliographical references and index.
  ISBN: 978-0-7456-2280-4 — ISBN: 978-0-7456-2281-1 (pbk)
  1. Friendship. I. Title. II. Series.
BF575.F66 P34 2000
302.3'4—dc21   00-035983

Typeset in 10.5 on 12 pt Plantin
by SetSystems, Saffron Walden, Essex
Printed and bound in Great Britain by Marston Book Services Limited, Oxford

This book is printed on acid-free paper.

For further information on Polity, visit our website: www.polity.co.uk

Contents

I dedicate this book to the memory of
Helen Sanders
1947–1999

From quiet homes and first beginning,
Out to the undiscovered ends,
There's nothing worth the wear of winning,
But laughter and the love of friends.

Hilaire Belloc

Preface

Writing more than a few lines of acknowledgements in a preface to a short book might seem pretentious. Yet I was forced to pause, recognizing that naming some who are in my personal community but not others would say something about me, about those I mentioned and about those I did not mention. I greatly enjoy reading other authors' prefaces. Some attempt to be gracious but are often patronizing. Others may attempt to be witty or detached but in their failure appear coy or laboured. The current vogue for reflexivity can provoke embarrassing self-revelations or cringe-making jovial self-consciousness.

A preface may allow the reader to glimpse something of the private person behind the public author, and one may gain insights that require more effort to decipher from the main text. Friends are conventionally perceived as adding to the quality of our lives. Few would readily own up to being friendless: it might suggest that they were misanthropic or lonely and less adequate as social beings. So maybe my own experience will in some way be reflected in the book, however hard I try to be objective. What I choose to include or exclude surely reflects my subjective judgement.

A peculiar privilege of the preface is that it is not generally considered to be within a reviewer's scope. Since the private is allowed ascendancy over the public, some more or less subtle disarming is possible. So, in the hope of avoiding toe-curling confessions, being neither self-important nor psychologically oppressive to the friend-challenged, I may be able to interest readers in the following remarks.

Throughout my life I have been fortunate in my friends – when I was younger they were mainly men; latterly they are likely to be women. For those seeking the roots of an author's experience and stance, let me reveal that I was sent off to boarding school at the age of eight and one or two close friends at school served as the family I did not see for months on end. At most later stages of my life I acquired new friends, and I have known a few of them longer than I knew my father.

Perhaps seeing the world through the eyes of different friends from diverse social and cultural backgrounds provides a good training for a sociologist. Those I know who themselves have a diverse set of friends often appear more receptive to objective analyses of social interaction. They are more likely to own up to the enjoyment of people-watching.

In my early years as a sociologist I was encouraged to recognize the instrumental importance of friends and friendship. The culture of my department at the University of Kent at Canterbury in the 1960s was grounded in the social anthropology of the Mediterranean countries. Gifts, exchange, reciprocity, patron–client relations and social networks were the stock-in-trade of our weekly graduate seminars. The young Mediterraneanists brought together by Paul Stirling knew that, when they went to southern Italy, southern Spain, Greece or Turkey, their first task was to listen to the gossip.

We discussed cronyism, 'corruption' and the Mafia. An anthropological study, published a few years previously, about the social connections and backgrounds of those investigated by the tribunal concerned with a leak of an impending change in the bank rate helped us to close the social distance between southern Italy and the City of London. I remember one seminar on the idea of a power elite during the year when George Homans was visiting professor from Harvard. In the discussion we asked him if, in his view, the term had significance in the United States. 'Of course there's no power elite in America', he thundered in his naval captain's voice. 'I know, because they are all my friends.'

It is perhaps not surprising, therefore, that I began writing about the importance of friends over thirty years ago. I also gave lectures on a course on the principles of social interaction where we focused on the writings of Georg Simmel and Erving Goffman. I hope that some of the students who attended that course will come across this book, perhaps through their own children who are now at university; or perhaps, in coming to terms with the loss or departure of a partner or a close friend, they recognize again the importance of friends in their lives.

It is so easy for prefaces to be self-indulgent. However, it is a pleasurable obligation to acknowledge the help I have received during the months spent writing this book. My daughter-friend, Kate Pahl, together with Claire Wallace, Paul Thompson and Liz Spencer, have provided stimulation in many discussions, as have, in their different ways, Julie Ford, Gillian Lello and Val Littlehales. Liz Spencer and Graham Allan very helpfully read the book in draft but are, of course, absolved from any responsibility for the final version. Liz Spencer and I are working on a joint research project at the University of Essex which, we hope, will help to clarify and test some of my ideas that still lack firm empirical support. She remains sceptical of some of my assumptions: I am very fortunate in being able to work with a colleague and friend of over twenty years' standing who maintains a steady eye on the evidence, without completely banning the exciting, if undisciplined, brainstorming that we both enjoy. Creative writing and research should be fun.

Finally, I would like to thank Rebecca Harkin, my supportive editor at Polity Press, Jenifer Tucker, whose consummate word-processing skills are beyond praise, and the staff of the Research Resources Unit at the Institute for Social and Economic Research at the University of Essex, who chased and found so many elusive references for me. It would be hard to imagine a more congenial supportive research base this side of the Atlantic.

However, for the author the best thing about a preface is that, after writing the last sentence, he can answer those around the town who ask him how the book is going, 'I have just finished it – come round for a drink.'

RAY PAHL
Bishop's Castle
Shropshire

Introduction

Friendship may be seen as an increasingly important form of social glue in contemporary society. Young adolescents are well known to be heavily dependent on their peers for social support and self-identity, but now more people are culturally determined by their friends until much later in life. The early friend-dependent phase seems to be continuing through their twenties and thirties for an increasing proportion of the population, and, for the minority without partners, friends remain central throughout their lives.

The word 'friend' in English can cover a wide range of close informal relationships, so that its use without qualification can be highly ambiguous. The invitation to bring a friend to an exhibition may imply little more than knowing what name to write in the book at the entrance. At the other extreme, a special friend can share one's deepest thoughts, hopes and fears and provide 'another self' to share the vicissitudes of life. Something of the range of the forms and types of friendship will be explored throughout this book. It would be helpful if the reader is watchful for his or her taken-for-granted assumptions about what makes a friend a friend, recognizing that, whatever these may be, they are not universally shared. As the social and cultural context of friendship changes over time, so does the meaning of what it is to be a friend.

Those in the Western world who so avidly watch the TV soap opera *Friends* pick up new styles and modes of friendship, as well as finding that the actors resonate with their own experiences. The TV drama both reflects and creates modern forms of friendship.

Sociologists claim that, in modern Western societies, there is a growing centrality of personal communities as opposed to geographical or work-based communities. These personal communities may be geographically scattered and may change substantially as we move through the life-course. The teenager's 'need' for friends is of a different order from the 'need' of the socially isolated eighty-something. Our social convoy of significant others may change and fluctuate as we go through life.

The social *zeitgeist* of the early twenty-first century is democratic, anti-authoritarian and egalitarian. Family relationships are, inevitably, hierarchical, reflecting the differences between generations and the birth-order of siblings. Sociologists have shown that our social relationships with members of our families are heavily dependent on whether or not we get on with them. Family obligations, duties and responsibilities will be affected by whether we actually like the people concerned. While this has probably always been the case, people are more ready to acknowledge their preferences in their mix of chosen kin and non-kin friends.

The growth of an egalitarian ideology between partners means that these, too, are self-consciously more friend-like. Indeed, marriages and partnerships can break up as much through the finding of another more sympathetic, supportive and understanding friend as through refocused desire. Many women will be much more likely to be influenced by their closest female friend than by their mother-in-law – or even their own parents. Some commentators have gone so far as to see the emergence of 'families of choice' – a phrase that originated in the gay community but which adds potency to the idea of personal communities.

This putative centrality of friends and friendship in contemporary society could be an important ingredient in the understanding of emerging social forms. The styles and symbols of contemporary culture are increasingly mediated through friends. Magazines of style and fashion are now more likely to surround their target consumers with friends, not family. The advertisement for Renault cars which showed a stylish father and daughter in collusion over their respective love lives is based on the assumption that the two are equals in their devotion to style. The young woman, Nicole, refers to her 'Papa' in a fond, sisterly, friend-like way. This is an exception that proves the rule: it nevertheless affirms that traditionally hierarchical relationships can be egalitarian and friend-like.

This modern focus on friends provides a challenge to conventional, traditional thinking about family and communities. Indeed, it was by my attempt to demythologize the idea of community that I was led to develop my interest in friends and friendship.

Over the last twenty or so years governments in the West have been increasingly concerned with social cohesion. Faced with rapidly rising divorce rates, the growth of juvenile crime, the apparent declining influence of parental authority, widespread feelings of insecurity among the elderly, declining involvement in local government and a host of other gloomy statistics purportedly indicating social decline, governments turned to sociologists for help and advice. Unwilling to acknowledge directly that increasing dependence on market forces and consumption is insufficient in itself to promote social solidarity, governments have responded to the beguiling promises of what has come to be known as 'communitarianism'.

The idea was encouraged in the United States of America in a book entitled *Habits of the Heart* (1985) by Robert Bellah and associates, which triggered off a debate about the decline of citizenship, moral responsibility and the relationship between character and society. These American social scientists, and many others who followed them, notably Amitai Etzioni, argued for the need for some kind of moral regeneration reflecting what Bellah et al. describe as 'the tremendous nostalgia many Americans have for the idealised "small town". The wish for a harmonious community . . . is a wish to transform the roughness of utilitarian dealings in the market place, the courts and government administration into neighbourly conciliation. But this nostalgia is belied by the strong focus of American individualism on economic success. The rules of the competitive market, not the practices of the town meeting or the fellowship of the church, are the real arbiters of living.'

Ever since the Old Testament prophets, and probably before, there have always been those who have inveighed against the decadence of contemporary society, contrasting it with a more integrated and cohesive society in the past. There are many contemporary voices bemoaning the so-called breakdown of the family through divorce and the labour market pressures related to the intensification of work and the associated insecurities and stresses that impinge deleteriously on 'family life'. Likewise, social and geographical mobility, the decline of traditional industries and the development of new services more dependent on female labour have disrupted or broken down 'traditional' communities. However, there are other contemporary voices that question the cosiness of previous putative golden ages. Feuds between neighbours and families led to much bitterness, mistrust and, indeed, physical violence. The simmering hatreds of the former Yugoslavia are seen to be more typical of traditional than modern societies. Those sceptical of the warmth, trust and communal responsibility of times past see the freely chosen friend as the basis for a new form of social morality. As I shall argue below in Chapter 2, friendships in the early modern period were more likely to be calculative exchange relationships than the mutual meeting of minds and spirits described in one way by Aristotle and in another by contemporary friend-focused people, such as the young woman discussed on pages 70–74 below.

There can be no going back, either to the authoritarian and patriarchal family, or to communities of deprivation and isolation. Isolated mining communities had certain strengths in their solidarities, but they also had material deprivation and female subservience. Unquestionably, twenty-first-century society is held together by qualitatively and quantitatively different social bonds from those more typical 300 years ago.

The crucial issue for those concerned with managing, governing and creatively understanding contemporary society is to know what, if anything, is replacing kinship obligations, civic responsibility and the mutual care and reciprocities engendered by being trapped in communities of fate. Evidently, strong social bonds do exist in some form, since the atomization of mass society based on individualized consumption is, in itself, an unlikely basis for social order. Whether or not these contemporary social bonds are becoming more firmly based on friends and friendship is an issue of fundamental importance.

Yet, perhaps surprisingly, there has been remarkably little scholarly concern with contemporary patterns and styles of friendship. This may be due partly to the fact that, as we shall see, the term 'friend' is notoriously difficult to define and friendship is famously difficult for the authorities to tame or to control. The rights, obligations and duties of 'next-of-kin' can be clearly specified in family law in a way not so easily extended to 'best friend'.

Given the difficulties involved in advocating a return to the world we have lost, there is a need to understand the new basis for social connectedness. A widely held assumption, for which there is much empirical support, is that those societies which have better organized reciprocities and civic solidarity also have better schools, faster economic growth, better health and well-being and more effective government. The precise social mechanisms which underlie such correlations are not yet very clear. However, it is commonly agreed that a discussion of these issues is helpfully advanced under the umbrella of a new term – *social capital*. Robert Putnam has defined social capital as referring to 'features of social organisation such as networks, norms, and social trust that facilitate co-ordination and co-operation for mutual benefit.'

Defining, exploring and expanding the notion of social capital keeps many contemporary social scientists very busy, and, happily, there is no need to go into the complex niceties of their work here. It will suffice for present purposes for readers to be aware that a common ingredient in most discussions of social capital is the further notion of social network or social support. Friends and friendship are assumed to be part of any individual's salient social circle.

The term 'social network' is frequently taken to be a more precise way of describing social connectedness. The term has been much used and abused. Often people say they are 'networking' when all they are doing is adding new contacts to their address books. However, the analogy of a network carries with it the notion of interconnectedness. Thus, a family may be described as a social network since, presumably, all members of a family know each other. If one were representing links diagrammatically, with each individual represented as a dot on a piece of paper, then lines representing linkages could be drawn between each of the dots, providing a very close-knit network. However, even though each member of the family might be aware of each other member, it need not follow that the nature of the links is uniform. Some may be closer and see each frequently; others may simply be aware of a tenuous tie of very minor social significance. The intensity, durability and other various qualitative and quantitative aspects of these linkages can be described or adduced.

Other social networks are more loose or ephemeral. Students at college may have a group of friends or acquaintances, some of whom know each other and others who do not. Some friends may know the parents or siblings of the person on whom the network is focused, others not. The student concerned may have a home-based network, a college-based network and later a work-based network, and so on. Careful analyses of these networks can become highly complex and, indeed, mathematically sophisticated. It will be evident that gathering the necessary information in order to carry out such network analyses can be hugely time-consuming and expensive. Understandably, perhaps, the quantitative analyses cannot explore the subtle nuances of each particular social relationship and the systems of classification have to be somewhat crude. Individuals may be designated simply as 'friends', 'neighbours', 'family', and so on. The fact that there are different kinds of friends is rarely considered, although, taking a crude index such as frequency of visiting, the relative importance of friends or family, *based on that criterion alone*, can be assessed. Thus, it can be shown in relation to various practical matters, such as finding a job, caring for or minding young children or being cared for when ill or very elderly, whether the help or support is more likely to be provided by friends or family. Such information is of interest, even though the precise definition of a friend – as opposed to other forms of social connectedness – remains elusive.

We shall return to a discussion of friendship and social capital later, in Chapter 5. My purpose now is simply to indicate how and why friends and friendship have come to have considerable contemporary, practical and theoretical importance.

Basically, it seems likely that two quite distinct processes are taking place at the same time. On the one hand, friends may be taking over various social tasks, duties and functions from family and kin, simply out of practical necessity. Those who move away to new areas may do all they can to keep in touch with the family they leave behind. However, despite frequent visits, phone calls, e-mails, letters, and so on, in an emergency and for much day-to-day support, there can be no substitute for geographical propinquity. Caring for a sick child who has to be collected from school in an emergency almost certainly requires the help of a local friend. As women's participation in the labour force continues to rise, so grandmothers and aunts as well as mothers are torn by other responsibilities. The problems of distance and availability remain. There is increasing survey evidence to support the growing practical importance of friends.

The second process is the changing meaning of friendship. Our ideas of what it means to be a good friend, a close friend, a really close friend or a best friend are changing. Our expectations and aspirations are growing, and we are even prepared to judge the quality of our relationships with kin on the basis of some higher ideal of whether we can be closer to them as friends. This putative change in the meaning and quality of friendship is much harder to measure, since people themselves are only recently coming to terms with these changes and recognizing their significance. Evidently, it is hard to get coherent information from people about something which they are barely aware exists.

Some of these difficulties will become more apparent in later chapters. I have begun researching on these problems with my colleague Liz Spencer at the University of Essex. The research project ends in 2001, so that publications are unlikely to appear before 2002 at the earliest, and it would be very unwise of me to suggest now any possible conclusions or outcomes. However, one thing can be said with certainty from the first round of interviews already completed. Respondents have little difficulty in describing their own personal communities and in recognizing that friends can be described as having different degrees of importance and significance for them at different stages of their lives. Some older respondents describe certain friends as being closer to them than their parents at later stages in the life-course. Some have special friends that mean more to them than anything else in life. Others have difficulty in recognizing any close friends at all. The diversity of ethnography with which we are faced presents daunting problems of analysis, but we are already convinced that we are documenting something of singular significance for understanding the changing basis of social connectedness in contemporary society. We use the term 'social convoy' to describe the fluctuating form of an individual's personal community as he or she moves through life.

One of the dominant arguments in contemporary social and cultural theory relates to the relative weight of cultural and economic determinants of social action and social identity. On the one hand are those who see us as still fundamentally determined by our economic inheritance and position in the labour market. According to this theoretical position, our life-chances and view of the world are determined by our fundamental material circumstances. While not all would use the term 'social class', there is a strong commitment to an underlying social structure that is determined by property and market relations. Other theorists, while not completely rejecting such a view, put greater emphasis on the cultural aspects of style and consumption. Identities are seen to be more fluid and flexible as people disregard or disguise their social origins, and the more rigid aspects of the division of labour are now claimed to be undermined and modified by the homogenizing influences of the mass media and mass consumption.

Focusing on friends and friendship can throw light on this debate. Are people's most important forms of social connectedness outside the family entirely unrelated to property, wealth and the occupational structure? Is true friendship free from the exigencies of material circumstances or does like attract like as they confirm and reaffirm each other's identities? Alternatively, are our friends determined culturally through similar interests and, likewise, do our friends help to define us culturally? As Graham Allan and Rebecca Adams recently remarked: 'our friends, in numerous ways, challenge our pretensions and evaluate our claims, all the while confirming our personal and structural identity. Through such validation of the self, the significance of friendship in binding the "bricks of social structure" together can be readily recognised. So just as friendships take on characteristics of the cultural, economic and social settings in which they arise, equally those ties are consequential in helping sustain the order there is within these settings.'

This puts a complex position rather well, and we return

to the question of identity in Chapter 3. The same authors argue strongly that friendship is likely to grow in salience. Informal solidarity, based on friendship, may well become more important by providing the necessary cement to hold the bricks of an increasingly fragmented social structure together.

In brief outline, the structure of the book is as follows: Chapter 1 explores in a general way the idea of friendship as it developed from its early beginnings in the Judeo-Christian writings and the ancient classics of Aristotle, Cicero and others. An attempt is made to describe a distinctive form of friendship, which emerged for perhaps 200 years in medieval Christendom. This opens up a number of issues that are taken up later. Chapter 2 is concerned with describing a distinctive form of friendship associated with the development of market society and emphasizes the crucial importance of trust in modern friendship. In Chapter 3 the friendship of modernity is linked with some of the recent philosophical interpretations of classical friendship and the inevitable question of how heterosexual friends and soul-mates can remain so, without also being lovers. The main contributions of sociology and social psychology to the study of friendship over the life-course are discussed rather critically in Chapter 4. Seemingly, the more social scientists attempt to analyse friendship, the more it somehow slips between their fingers. We return to the study of social capital, social support and social engineering in Chapter 5. It is suggested that friendship binds and undermines at the same time and that the distinction between the public and the private needs to be strongly observed and maintained. Failure to recognize this distinction may lead to serious unintended consequences. The current fashion in management education, for example, emphasizing the importance of networking could, in another sphere, easily become cronyism. Finally, the book concludes in a more speculative way about some of the implications and interconnections evident in the previous five chapters.

Friendship is sure to grow in social and political importance as traditional forms of social glue decline or are modified. Friendships of hope could be seen as a metaphor for an enduring twenty-first-century morality.

1

What is Friendship?

The outlook which values the collective above the
individual necessarily disparages friendship; it is a
relation between men at their highest level of individuality . . . to say 'these are my friends' implies
'those are not'.

C. S. Lewis, *The Four Loves*

God is friendship.

Aelred of Rievaulx

In contemporary Western society we choose our friends
to form part of our private life. They can, it is true,
impinge on public life when they are used to acquire
favours or personal advancement but, while it is recognized that this occurs, the assumption is that such behaviour is not normatively acceptable. Our friends are
personal to us and we are not obliged to be friends of our
friends' friends. Hence the term 'friendship network' may
be misleading, except in those circumstances where those
in a given set do have friendly relations with all the others
in the set to a greater or lesser extent. We choose our
friends and reciprocally they choose us, although the
relative balance of commitment and affect may not be
known by either actor in the dyad.

Unlike the relations between family and kin, there is no

formal institutional support, such as family law, to keep friends together or to sanction various duties and obligations. There is, to be sure, some social odium attached to those who exploit friends – the spongers and cads – who abuse hospitality, ignore reciprocities and substitute superficial charm for genuine social engagement. While there is little common agreement on what counts as being a true friend, a real mate or buddy, people will respond to given actions and behaviours by emphasizing and appreciating their quality: 'She was there when I needed her.' 'He was a really good friend.' However, there is no common agreement on any kind of qualitative scale. The notion of 'best friend' can be interpreted in different ways.

People do not generally set out to move up any such scale of friendship: to be so calculating would seem to undermine its spontaneous and voluntary character. The quality of the friendly act is often perceived only in retrospect, when the context can be seen in perspective. Similarly, some friends are more likely to fade away – often encouraged by social or geographical mobility – and are rarely formally 'dumped'. Friendship exists largely through an involvement in certain activities, which generates sentiments which, in turn, encourage further activities.

Such iteration between sentiments and activities may be specific to particular contexts and stages in the life-course. Our time at school, in periods of training or further education, our early experience of employment, the stage of being heavily involved with young children, or in retirement and in old age – these and other stages and contexts may generate their own distinctive set of friends. Some of these fall away as we go through life; others are remembered at Christmas or perhaps at birthdays, and yet others are maintained with some effort through visits, letters, telephone calls and now e-mail.

A further theme of this book is that friend-like relations

may exist among kin. Some people, it is tru
experienced either social or geographical mυ___ _
likely that they went to school with most of those friends
they may have outside their family and also that, in their
kinship circle, they are closer to some than others. This
suffusing of kin links with the norms and expectations of
friendship makes a peculiarly strong social bond. There
are, of course, certain social expectations associated with
the roles of sibling or cousin but when warm, friendly
feelings are superimposed, a qualitatively different kind of
social form emerges. Friendly relations of this sort may
also change through the life-course, depending on behaviours and activities connected with the care and support
of elderly parents and other relatives or perhaps conflicts
over inheritance. Many readers might find these statements unremarkable, but it is important not to forget that
the degree of openness, permissiveness and freedom of
choice which we may take for granted does not apply to
all societies and to all historical periods.

To make contemporary assumptions more vivid I turn
next to describe a scene from a recent novel. This brings
alive and makes more accessible, perhaps, something of
the contemporary world of friendship among a particular
urban cohort at the end of the twentieth century. I then
whisk the reader rather sharply back to the ancient world,
where friendships of which we have knowledge are mainly
between men. The invisibility of women's friendships
should not lead to an unwarranted assumption that they
did not exist.

One of the most enduring and, indeed, provocative
accounts of friendship was provided by Aristotle. His
attempt to distinguish a qualitatively superior form of
friendship remains highly contentious but still serves to
bother philosophers, who wrestle with its meaning and
implications.

In order to provide some insight into a pre-modern form of friendship, of which there is a surprising amount of documentation, I draw on monastic sources of the eleventh and twelfth centuries. This is, of course, limited to men who are mostly celibate. Without their own families of procreation, friendship provided effective and instrumental ties that would otherwise be missing. I return to the modern view of friendship at the end of the chapter.

Thirty-something friendship:
a literary vignette

Frankie Blue is an estate agent. Now aged thirty, he has a degree in politics and philosophy from the University of West Middlesex (formerly Staines Technical College) and is forming a relationship with Veronica, who is a pathologist. One evening Frankie observes her inspecting a very large 5' x 5' collage of snapshots, which he put together in a frame after his father died a year previously: 'Every time I look at it I see something new, some lost friend I had forgotten, some distant moment I had lost. Living is all forgetting and remembering. The board had the power to draw out of you the invisible, the missing, the irretrievably broken. It was all in bits, but it made up a whole. And the bits were bits of me, every single one of them.' Frankie felt that all new relationships involved trying to steal the past of the other, and he comes to stand by Veronica, who asks questions about the subject of various photographs. He looks at his past with fresh eyes: 'So dozens, scores of faces stare back at me, faces with whom I have laughed, and shared secrets, and drunk, and played stupid games, and, in my way, loved. Gone most of them. Married with mortgages in Weston-super-Mare. Working for software companies abroad. Can't talk or won't talk.

Fallen out or fallen away. Good friends I haven't seen for years, not only through geography but through natural erosion.'

Frankie's thoughts in the early pages of Tim Lott's novel *White City Blue* are a prelude to its main theme, which is the tension Frankie feels between loyalty to his friends and his new-found love. Friends, he suspects, are 'your accumulated history. One way or another they hold you up, they remind you who you are, insist on who it is you remain. That can be interesting too. Old friends can be like deadwood, like one of those petrified forests. You have to fight your way through, not in order to get anywhere, just to stay in the present, just not to get dragged back into the past.'

Frankie is scared of the idea of 'relationship' – even the word makes him 'think of a boat-load of relatives'. Veronica asks him how many friends he has in all.

> I have no idea. I know of quite a few. More than the average 30-year old, I should imagine. The average would be . . . what? Ten really good ones. Ten more peripheral. A score or so right at the outside edge, virtual acquaintances. A few left over from school, a few more from college, a few picked up at work, perhaps an ex in there somewhere. One or two borrowed or stolen from other friends. An ex-flatmate or two. Not as many mates as I used to have, that's for sure.

Having started on this more systematic and objective analysis of what we shall call in this book his *personal community*, Frankie realizes how loosely he is using the word friend:

> I'm not sure what a friend is. Is it just someone you like? Can it be someone you haven't seen for ten years and have no intention of seeing again? Do friends expire? What's the

difference between a friend and an acquaintance? It's very hard to say.

Veronica interrupts Frankie's musings with practical questions about who should be invited to the wedding. She offers to help Frankie by dividing his friends into types and sticking coloured pins into the separate varieties. He imagines that she is joking but decides to play along. He starts to name the varieties.

For a start there are friends you don't like. I've got plenty of those. Then there are friends you do like, but never bother to see. Then there are the ones you really like a lot, but can't stand their partners. There are those that you just have out of habit and can't shake off. Then there's the ones you're friends with not because you like them, but because they are very good-looking or popular and it's kind of cool to be their friend. Trophy friends. Most of the time that's what I call VCSPs, although you can be a trophy friend without being a VCSP. It's just that the two tend to go together.

What does VCSP stand for?

Very Charming, Selfish People. I've got two of them, and a third border line. They hold you on a string. Then when they feel you're getting far enough out for the string to break, they pour the charm on, draw you back in again. Make you feel that you're the only person in the world. For about 10 minutes. Then when that's done, they let go again, because other people's strings need drawing in. They go for quantity rather than quality. They need the fix, the drama. They need to . . . beguile people so that they can feel real

[. . .]

Then there are sports friends. There are friends of convenience – they're usually work friends. There are pity friends who you stay with because you feel sorry for them. There are acquaintances who are on probation as friends. There are – .

At this point Frankie feels irritated by his self-conscious and clinical categorization and wants to stop. Veronica persists by pointing out that some clear-cut criteria are needed to decide who should be invited to the wedding and who not. Would those not invited be offended? Would that matter? And so on.

The pair of them then set about sticking differently coloured pins into the photos of Frankie's friends. Veronica has a good time putting yellow pins into Frankie's ex-girlfriends. In the end there are only blue pins left in the box. 'How about making that for the untouchables?' said Veronica. 'You know, the blue chip chums, the friends who are beyond criticism, who you would trust with your life, who would stand by you and so on and so forth.'

Frankie mentions three and Veronica is not convinced. It's because Frankie does not really understand the full complexity of different forms of friendship that Veronica is proved right and he wrong. It takes a full-length novel for Frankie's shift in understanding about friendship to come about.

The book has been hailed as one of the very best portrayals of male friendship ever written. This is evident hyperbole but it is also rather paradoxical, since it is clear, as the novel unfolds, that Frankie has a more limited view of friendship than that developed in the classical tradition to which we refer below.

Certainly there is a conventional stereotype that men are all rather like Frankie and, sadly, are not able to enjoy the complex, communicative friendships which women more readily claim. Sociologists would be quick to add historical context, stage in the life-course and social class to the somewhat simplistic gender differences portrayed in the novel. Discussions and analyses of friendship have a long and distinguished history. Some reference to this tradition will help to put later discussions in context.

Friendship in the ancient world

The close, communicative friendships of antiquity of which we have knowledge were between men in patriarchal societies. One such case, the friendship between David and Jonathan, is described in the Second Book of Samuel. The love that Jonathan showed David was not appropriately reciprocated. We are told that 'Jonathan loved him as his own soul', and the Bible makes clear that his friendship was stronger than loyalty to his father, loyalty to the king and his own personal ambitions. When David hears of Jonathan's death, David eulogizes:

> Wonderful was thy love to me
> Passing the love of women.

There is some debate as to whether David truly related to Jonathan with equal whole-heartedness.

Certainly, from the earliest times, philosophers and others have struggled to extract the essence of what would make an ideal, true, real or perfect friendship. Bidipai has been quoted as saying, around 326 BC:

> Honest men esteem and value nothing so much in this world as a real friend. Such a one is, as it were, another self, to whom we impart our most secret thoughts, who partakes our joy, and comforts us in our affliction; add to this that his company is an everlasting pleasure to us.

In this ideal, true, reciprocal friendship there is affection, respect and loyalty and it has been claimed that 'one friend in a lifetime is much; two are many; three are hardly possible'. Such friendships were not possible in the past between men and women – or, if they were, we have no knowledge of them – when the status of women was so much inferior to that of men. There were, of course, exceptions. Equality of status is a necessary condition for a reciprocal friendship.

It is quite clear, as Frankie Blue so neatly reminds us, that there are friends and friends. Perhaps the most famous discussion is that by Aristotle, who distinguished between friends of utility, friends of pleasure and friends of virtue. According to him, it is only the last that establishes a relationship between whole persons. A useful way to understand the differences between the first two and the third is to make a distinction between activity and process, which Aristotle discusses in the *Metaphysics*. A nice way of seeing this distinction is put forward by Suzanne Stern-Gillet in her book *Aristotle's Philosophy of Friendship*. She points out that it can be correctly said of a nun in meditation that she is both meditating and has meditated, since meditation or contemplation is an activity. However, if the same nun was cooking a meal it cannot be said at any one time that she was cooking and has cooked. Cooking is a process, whereas contemplation is an activity.

Friendships of utility and pleasure may be compared to processes – such friends may help us to move house or play tennis with us – whereas the primary friendship of virtue is an activity – simply that of being a soul-mate. Philosophers still find much to discuss in understanding the true notion of friendships of virtue (see pages 80–86 below for a comparison of the mirror and secrets view of friendship). Aristotle's view of friendships of virtue suggest that this is one of the essential ingredients of the good life:

> To perceive a friend, therefore, is necessarily in a manner to perceive oneself, and to know a friend is in a manner to know oneself.

The excellent person is related to his friend in the same way as he is related to himself, since a friend is another himself.

Virtuous friends enlarge and extend each other's moral experience. The friends are bound together, becoming, as it were, each other, as they recognize each other's moral excellence. Each can be said to provide a mirror in which the other may see himself. It may thus be claimed that this pure Aristotelian form of friendship constitutes the most complete moral experience of which a human being is capable. The combination of the loving perception of individuals with the apprehension of their virtue helps us to achieve the good life.

Friendship derives its moral significance both from the choice that presides at its formation and from the virtues involved in its cultivation. To that extent it signals a concordance between reason, passion and desire.

However, if friendship has all these imputed moral benefits, could it be that we love our friends as much for securing benefits to ourselves as for their own sakes. If we love our friend for her own sake and not just for what she is, that would imply that one would further her interests at the expense of our own. Such a friendship would then impose moral obligations upon us. In a perfect friendship, each partner makes the other the end of his activities as a friend. Modern accounts of people's 'best friend' emphasize the importance of being accepted simply for what you are.

Early writings on friendship are scarce. There are many references to friends and friendship in the Bible which can provide some clues, albeit one stage removed from actual empirical accounts. The friendship between David and Jonathan, already mentioned, the misery of Job when his friends deserted him and references to the dangers of having treacherous friends are common in the writings of Jeremiah and Zechariah and elsewhere. The various folk sayings and tribal wisdom gathered together in the Proverbs provide some clues to the normative expectation of friends. Seemingly, Old Testament friends needed resources in order to engage in reciprocal exchanges. The poor suffered – as ever – from social exclusion and the rich had greater social capital.

> The poor is hated even of his own neighbour: but the rich hath many friends. (Proverbs 14: 20; an alternative translation would be 'many are the lovers of the rich'.)

A later proverb makes clear that friendship is more instrumental than affective ('Wealth maketh many friends; but the poor is separated from his neighbour', 19: 4).

Such an idea of friendship based on differential wealth and status, and presumably rooted in some kind of patron–client relationship, does not seem particularly egalitarian. Hence the teaching of Jesus in the New Testament appears liberating, if not revolutionary. The injunction to 'love thy neighbour as thyself' would, if acted upon, create a more widely suffused friendly society. In the parable of the woman who lost one of her pieces of silver, Jesus illustrates her happiness at finding it by describing the way she threw a party for her friends and neighbours in celebration (Luke 15: 9). The man who found the sheep that was lost similarly called together his friends and neighbours for collective celebration. This idea of a partying style of affective friendship must have been already in existence, as there is no implication that Jesus was referring to an unfamiliar mode of behaviour. It is, however, perhaps surprising that the conventional phrase was 'friends and neighbours' rather than 'family and friends', although, as we shall see below, in many societies the terms family and friends are synonymous. Jesus in more prophetic mode, describing the likely fortunes of the early church, is quoted by St Luke as saying:

> Ye shall be betrayed both by parents, and brethren, and kinsfolks, and friends; and some of you shall they cause to be put to death. (21: 16)

It is not necessary to go into the intricacies of biblical exegesis and textual criticism to discover the impact of scriptural writings on the behaviour of men and women in the first millennium. Literary sources are evidently limited, but a lively interest in friendship appeared to emerge among the monastic communities, and there is some reference to it in Anglo-Saxon poetry.

Friendship in pre-modern Europe

The literature of men's friendship increased in the last half of the eleventh century and in the first decades of the twelfth century. The main source is the collection of letters in monasteries and new secular centres of learning. The growth of monastic and cathedral schools from the end of the tenth century helped to produce a new, literate, intellectual and largely celibate elite, much excited by the writings of Cicero on friendship and concerned to explore secular and spiritual love as part of a wider project of understanding human relationships. For example, Gerbert of Aurillac, who became Pope Sylvester II (999–1003), while never a monk, well understood the monastic tradition, and wrote a series of letters when he was a teacher at Rheims in the 980s. Gerbert was a political climber who recognized the usefulness of friends for influence, patronage and favours. He used his friends and used his network instrumentally to obtain books and so forth and supported his friends in their applications for jobs, such as an appointment as a teacher of music at a monastery. This would be termed cronyism today but it also reflects bonds of loyalty and affection.

Gerbert's wily use of friendship for his own career advancement made him view it in a secular way as a generalized social bond. For him it was essential social glue, a practical social element that made the world go round – not because individuals love each other as friends but because he felt communities function better through the harmony that friendship provides. This is a view of friendship clearly traceable to Cicero. He saw it as a source of order in society but at the same time as a social relationship that is more frequently sought than found. In a statement more appropriate, perhaps, to the discourse of late modernity Gerbert wonders: 'From where would arise families, from where cities and kingdoms, unless stabilised by association and friendship?' This and other writings of Gerbert of Rheims have been published in German, and it may be surprising to those who are not scholars of the period to know how much complex and subtle writing about friends and friendship dates from the tenth to twelfth centuries. Clearly Gerbert used his ideas about instrumental friendship very successfully. He did not seem to be overly bothered about the role of friendship in Christian life.

As would be expected, monks were more focused on exploring, understanding and practising Christian friendship. Some believed that friendship endangered human salvation by distracting from the wholehearted love of God. In the words of St James: 'The friendship of the world is enmity with God.' A further problem that might be implicit, if not explicit, in monastic writings on friendship is the fear of homoerotic ties.

However, the development of the cathedral schools in the eleventh century consolidated a new and distinctive approach to friendship, seeing it as an important and valuable part of the Christian life. In some of the letters it is clear that friendship could be of practical use as well as being valued for its own sake. It seems that there was also a revival and renewal in the monastic expression of friendship at the end of the tenth century, particularly at Tegernsee in Bavaria and later at Chartres. However, it was the youths who attended the cathedral schools – whether monastic or secular – who were encouraged to practice their Latin by writing letters. Men were needed who could express themselves clearly and precisely so that they could draw up deeds and charters at courts or churches. While it is true that many of the letters express the standard elements of conventional medieval letters, scholars can nevertheless detect in some from this period indications of more direct human feelings and close social bonds.

In one group of letters from the cathedral school at Worms, it is clear that the writers were drawing on both classical and Christian concepts of friendship without contrasting or distinguishing between the two. Friendship was seen as a natural and essential human impulse that could quite appropriately be given a central place in a letter. Indeed, it could be said that friendship and letter-writing belonged together in the cathedral schools of the eleventh century. There is one significant letter from the Bishop of Worms to an apparently powerful superior of a women's monastery in which he defends spiritual love between men and women and then goes on to ask for a favour which she was in a position to grant because of her political influence. Such detailed letters are evidently more significant for understanding the realities of friendship than the more common formulaic ones.

An emerging job market for scholars encouraged ambitious clerics to use their networks and social capital to further their own and others' interests. The ideology of this old-monk network was articulated through an expression of friendship emphasizing the importance of trust and loyalty. Writers from Chartres, Worms and Hildesheim looked upon friendship as a manifestation of the normal and natural bonds that men have with each other in everyday life. Spiritual reflections gave way to practical job-hunting, and for this friends became essential. The new centres of learning kept in touch with each other in such a way that the importance and significance of friendship was intensified. This emerging society was, to a large degree, held together through the language and practice of friendship. Cicero's contribution to the understanding of friendship was kept alive by the scholar-clerics of the period.

It has been suggested that in the later eleventh century men's bonds with women in the religious life could be just as important as those of men with each other. However, while there are some convincing examples, there are not many. The period 1120–1180 has been termed 'the age of friends'. Among the arguments to support this claim are, firstly, the importance of the growth of the cathedral schools with their literary pursuits, which we have noticed. Secondly, a change in the spiritual conception of the relation to God which emphasized the saint more as a friend of God and supported a view of friendship that recognized the worth of human bonds as part of the scheme of salvation. Thirdly, the Gregorian reform movement heightened controversy and encouraged monks to choose sides, find allies and generate more collective bonding. Fourthly, because St Anselm, when a prior at Bec, continued to correspond with his monks after their departure to Canterbury, his letters encouraged other monks to write about interpersonal bonds. Finally, as a response to the social changes of the eleventh century friendship was a necessity for the youths in the cathedral schools. In order to make their way in a more competitive society, friends were essential to provide support and opportunities for geographical and social mobility.

Perhaps surprisingly there did not appear to be a great concern about homosexuality in clerical circles. The possibility that physical love might flow from close friendship does not appear in the eleventh-century literature of monastic friendship.

A common theme in twelfth century letters of friendship is an insistence on regular contact between friends to maintain the relationship. It seemed to be commonly accepted then that friendship is governed by certain laws, making it a predictable and dependable practice in society. Friends were expected to be open with each other about their needs. The letters of Peter of Celle illustrate well the Benedictine tradition of monastic friendship, revealing an abbot's friendship with other monks and with secular clerics. For him friendship, family and monastery were bound up together as one. Intelligent and articulate visitors to Celle discussed intellectual problems together, as well as spiritual matters, and strong friendships developed. As the author of the standard work on the topic remarked:

> When friends disagreed or let each other down, accusations came forward in force. Irony, bitterness and disappointment came to the surface. Twelfth century monastic friendships can at moments remind us of the nineteenth century marriages immortalised in the Swedish playwright Strindberg's plays dealing with the search for love and the numbing pain and bitter anger of unanswered love.

Peter's later letters to John of Salisbury drop the generally pervasive biblical language and imagery for more direct and informal expression. He reminded John of how they used to joke together about such things as the size of the reliquary of Thomas Becket or ironically complained of John unnecessarily apologizing for keeping a borrowed book when he, Peter, never doubted he would return it. These are chatty and affectionate letters which surely indicate close emotional bonds between such medieval churchmen.

Some of the letters which refer to kisses and embraces indicate the level of trust and intimacy that developed between these men. The more informal style of these letters reflects the warmth, completeness and centrality of this friendship. They also indicate why Peter felt so betrayed if his friends let him down. His letters were important to him and he asked his friend Abbot Bernered of Soissons to keep them for him. Perhaps Peter felt that he had expressed something important about his own self and identity in his correspondence which he wanted to be preserved.

It was, of course, unquestionably accepted that friendship should not disrupt the social cohesion of the monastic community. It is significant, and perhaps surprising, that Peter's letters show that he considered friendship between people of different rank and station to be possible – such as between a monk and his friend outside the community or between an abbot and his secretary or between an abbot and a bishop.

After about 1180 the great age of the Cistercian fathers drew to a close. The previous forms of friendship as a bond that enhanced community became less central. The discussion of friendship by Cicero came to be more salient: the spiritual aspect was more united with the practical aspects of friendship and the social capital that people thereby accumulate in order to get on in life was more readily discussed. Peter of Blois, Archdeacon of Berlin in the 1180s, wrote in one of his letters: 'Are not my friends my inner self, whom I cherish and who take care of me in a sweet commerce of services, in an identity of affection?' The language may be somewhat flowery, but Peter assumed that the bonds of friendship would provide him with the status and recognition he required as part of a cultivated life. The cronyism of the London clubs or of the Philadelphia gentleman has long antecedents. Friendship was both instrumental and affective: altruism and kindness were paralleled with mutual service and reciprocal support. Peter, and others at the time, maintained their friendships of youth, even after conversion to the monastic life. Friendship was becoming accepted as a natural human practice and not simply an element of the spiritual life.

Peter is a recognizable type, similar to the contemporary unemployed but aspiring academic who feels obliged to hustle, make contacts and take on lucrative contracts but at the same time wishes to maintain a sense of dignity and to receive appropriate respect for his talents from his peers. By writing about friendship as an ennobling feature in social life, Peter hoped to acquire merit by association: he was adept at reactivating what I term 'fossil friends' for his own purposes. By shifting towards a more utilitarian view of friendship, Peter could quickly put his theory into practice. So, in 1192, Peter reminded Conrad, Archbishop of Mainz, that since they had lived in the same residence hall as students a bond had developed which he tried to cash in by getting Conrad's support in getting King Richard released from captivity. This is an excellent example of attempting to utilize 'the strength of weak ties' (see page 149–51). Peter believed, perhaps, more in networking than in developing deep, communicative friendship.

Other letters of the period reflected practical concerns: there was a request in one for various seeds and plant cuttings; another mixes the stereotypical phrases of friend-ship with a practical request to help in buying lead for the church roof. With a more secular emphasis on friendships of utility, men were becoming much more ready to cash in on obligations of reciprocity. Friendship was moving in the late twelfth and early thirteenth century to involve a more 'modern' mode of segmented and multi-level relationships.

Cronyism and patronage were soon to flourish mightily in the secular world of the early Renaissance. The early thirteenth century Italian writer Boncompagno da Signa was master and teacher of rhetoric in Bologna and other Italian universities. In his *Amicitia*, written in 1205, he provides fascinating insights into the subtleties of the modes and patterns of social interaction in the Italian city states. In this new secular world the ideals of spiritual friendship were openly abandoned. Nor did Boncom-pagno bother much with the classical tradition of Aristotle and Cicero. Most of the twenty-nine different types of friendship he describes are forms of opportunism dis-guised as friendship. The interest of this work is that it gives insight into actual day-to-day relations. One of his types is the 'vocal friend', who uses the language of friendship but means none of it. There is the sponger who readily accepts hospitality and who when greeting his host in the street after some hospitality embraces him tenderly and says with a happy voice: 'Good that you have come, how are you? Is your wife in good health? And do your sons enjoy bodily health?' However, this insincere friend of the thirteenth century never reciprocates the hospitality, although he is always effusive in his offers when he is sure they are unlikely to be accepted: 'We really must have dinner together when you're next in town.' The type is truly modern!

Boncompagno's examples are curiously familiar and

illustrate well the superficiality and insincerity of the so-called friendships of colleagues, fellow parents and neighbours. It is all part of the presenting of our false selves, as the post-Freudian Karen Horney described them in *Neurosis and Human Growth*. Boncompagno describes the 'shady friends' – number twenty-three *de umbratili amico* – who provide favours until they have achieved what they want and then drop the relationship.

Boncompagno is better at unmasking cynical game-playing than in exploring the deeper nature of friendship which is part of the Aristotelian tradition. His approach is closer to Stephen Potter's development of the idea of 'one-upmanship'; he is realistic, urbane and pragmatic. He challenges friendship as being closely involved with the spiritual life. Close friendships may indeed exist but he is wary and sceptical. He echoes the title of a recent essay by the sociologist Diego Gambetta – 'Can We Trust Trust?'. He is interested in the way that spiritual relationships are commodified with the coming of a commercial secular society in early Renaissance Italy. It is hard to fit his witty and elegant debunking into the model of 'traditional society' which sociologists try to impose on the past. When Georg Simmel wrote that 'modern man' is unable to sustain friendship in the ancient sense because he has too much to hide, he was particularly vague about what he meant by modern. So, indeed, are most sociologists.

It may be reasonably objected that this discussion of friendship among celibate men of the intellectual and cultural elite of medieval Europe reveals little of how the mass of ordinary people, largely illiterate and subject to little objective observation by others, related to those outside their families. It might be assumed that friendship was a privilege limited to those with the time to enjoy it. However, in his study *Montaillou*, Le Roy Ladurie re-creates the life of a small village in the Pyrenees of about 250 people, where between 1318 and 1325 a detailed Inquisition took place, primarily to eliminate heresy. As a result of this, an immense amount of detailed ethnography has been preserved about the pattern of the village's social relationships. One of the shepherds in the village, Pierre Maury, appeared fairly independent, since he owned up to 100 sheep and some asses. He was a wage earner, free from the subsistence economy and also, largely, from feudalism. He could get his friends to look after his sheep when he went off to the town, and he enjoyed parties, entertainment or communal meals with his friends. These friends were based primarily on family relationships but he had a strong sense of fraternity not based on blood. These are the words he used, as reported by the Inquisitor:

> I love Guillaume more than any of my brothers; although I have four brothers in the flesh. For those who are of the faith practise concord in everything. So they are more one another's brothers than those born of the same father and mother in the flesh: such brothers are always quarrelling with one another! And I shall never let Guillaume down: for all that we possess we pool half and half.

Very often these very close friendships were not based simply on choice and affection but grew out of other family links, such as being a godparent (compère or commère). As Pierre was reproached by the Inquisitor:

> You make yourself many *compères* and *commères* because you take part in so many baptisms; you spend all you have in this kind of festivity; and yet these baptisms and compaternities are good for nothing except to establish friendships between people.

Pierre replies:

I will not give it up for you or for anyone else, because in
that way I acquire many people's friendship.

Since Pierre spent his life as a migrant, practising
transhumance with his flocks, he had many opportunities
to be invited to baptisms and to acquire fellow-sponsors
as friends. Pierre and his colleagues also established associations of shepherds, which served many practical purposes. So a whole circle of different forms of friends and
friendship emerged, from fraternal and compaternal to
just ordinary friendships, providing a social network of the
utmost importance – stronger, claims Ladurie, than in the
more individualistic societies of the modern world.

The women of *Montaillou* also expressed great solidarity
and friendship. There were well-established informal networks of women before the accusations of heresy encouraged them to close ranks. We are told that Béatrice de
Planissoles had at least five close women friends in Dalon
'in whom she could confide her secrets'.

Without detailed literary accounts of the everyday life
of ordinary people it is very hard to understand the
significance of their friendships. Throughout feudal
Europe groups were based on blood relationships,
described in France as *parenté* or *lignage*. However, kins-
folk in France were typically called *amis* (friends), whereas
those in Germany were *Freunde*. In an eleventh-century
legal document from the Ile de France, the enumeration
appears: 'His friends, that is to say his mother, his brother,
his sister and his other relatives by blood or by marriage.'
The general assumption appeared to be that friendship
existed only between persons united by blood. Similarly,
in Ireland in the 1930s 'relatives' and 'friends' were two
ways of describing the same people.

A comparable elision was true in England, where the
word 'friend' was used for relatives as well as non-relatives

until the eighteenth century. A person's 'friends' might include anyone from employees, guarantors, guardians or more distant relatives. Before people married they needed to obtain the 'goodwill', if not the formal consent, of such friends. However, in practice couples could still marry, whatever their 'friends' advised.

Towards a modern view of friendship

Modern conceptions of friendship are concerned more with fidelity, solidarity and trust than with the Aristotelian abstract values of the good, the fine and the rational. While not generally using the language of philosophy, people do recognize the idea of a 'soul-mate', even if individually they do not have one. In our research at the University of Essex, we asked respondents to place the twenty people who are closest to them in a set of concentric circles. Generally they had little difficulty in deciding which few go into the innermost circle in which they are, as it were, in the middle, and those who are graded further out. Without exception, those with partners would put their opposite number in the first circle.

Frankie in Tim Lott's novel thinks he has primary friends, but they appear to be friends of pleasure or utility. There are indications that Veronica has more experience of friendships of virtue, and Frankie may develop a different stance towards friendship if their conjugal relationship develops and deepens, based on trust and communication.

There is clearly a distinction between friends as people and friendship as a quality that can be shared with kin as much as with chosen others. The Aristotelian notion of a kind of pure friendship can have a spiritual quality, and this form of friend-like relationship may be restricted to siblings, or even to parents and children. When people have this kind of special relationship with a close friend, it can be the most meaningful relationship in their lives. There may now be some normative pressure to put one's partner into the category of 'best friend', but this is more problematic than it may first seem, as we shall see below. In traditional society, patterns of inequality or hierarchy in general prevented the development of friends of virtue among kin or spouses: deference to age or patriarchy inhibited the emergence of what Anthony Giddens has termed 'confluent', that is non-dependant, relationships.

People now distinguish between those kin with whom they have an affinity and those whom they find difficult or whom they may wish to avoid. Uncongenial kin can be socially relegated and soul-mates can be centrally import-ant in a person's life. An interesting question to explore would be whether our modern chosen friends siphon off, as it were, sentiments which were previously attached mainly to kin. Perhaps this is more likely among those with the means and leisure to cultivate and to sustain a further set of social obligations and reciprocities.

Among sociologists in the twentieth century the import-ance of friendship was, until very recently, largely disre-garded or considered to be of ephemeral importance, compared with the issues surrounding family, work and the life-course. Indeed, the century began with the power-ful assertion by the German sociologist Georg Simmel that modernity is inevitably destructive of friendship – in the sense used in classical debates. He argued that all the differentiating forces of modern life split us up into spe-cialized roles so that our distinctive cluster of roles is too uniquely individualized to be able to relate in a holistic way to another single person. The modern way of feeling, he suggested, produces differentiated friendships, imply-ing that we would have separate friends for particular interests and activities. We would lunch with one, play sport with another and complain about our partners to another. The assumption is that friends would respect the boundaries of these differentiated relationships: if they had common interests in travel and holidays, for example, they would not expect also to share their deepest thoughts about religion or their sexual proclivities. Such friends would not be expected or try to probe into the depths of a person's soul. For Simmel, the modern style of friendship would be based on reserve and discretion. Modern people have too much to hide.

Perhaps only in marriage might true, holistic intimacy emerge. Couples would develop a kind of intimacy more closely related to the ancient idea of friendship in its purest and most virtuous form as a defence against the modern tendencies of differentiation and fragmentation.

However, men and women do not find it very easy to achieve this ideal. It has been shown that for many women this sense of who they are and where they are going is better achieved through the close friendship of other women. The women's movement in the 1970s and 1980s supported women in conceptualizing the value of friendship. Any suggestion that female friends had to be given reduced significance when women were living with a partner was rejected. Women's friends were often portrayed by men as being less serious, as being frivolous and as being more an aspect of play. In response to such a patronizing attitude, many women turned to other women to help them achieve a greater sense of autonomy and individuality. What it means to be in a committed partnership or to be a mother was better explored with other women than with a husband, who might feel threatened, lack the capacity for what has been called emotional work or simply be physically absent or tired when most needed.

The modern idea of friendship lies in its very freedom from public roles and obligations. As Allan Silver remarks,

' "spouses, lovers, kin and colleagues are friends" to the extent that they treat the objective conditions of their bond as collateral or inessential.' Friendship, as a continuous creation of personal will and choice, is ungoverned by the structural definitions that bear on family and kinship. This, then, is the ideal, but, as many sociologists have shown in their empirical research, most people's friendships do have clear boundaries of obligations. Thus, if respondents are asked to whom they would turn if they were in financial difficulties, few would mention a friend. In the case of difficulties in connection with a partner relationship, more would mention friends, particularly those who are younger and still in touch with the friends they had before entering a relationship. Older people whose relationship is faltering might confide in a sibling or a 'best friend', but at this stage many would not want to burden or worry those from their family of origin or family of procreation. Sometimes friends would not be approached for advice lest what they say may be 'too sensible'. Disregarding such advice might then affect the future course of the relationship. This suggests a positive reluctance to put the ideal of friendship to the test.

The shared conception of a common *ideal* of modern friendship makes the empirical reality difficult to discover without careful and quite subtle methods of observation and analysis. Thus, for example, a woman might feel obliged to claim that her partner is also her best friend. Her response to an interviewer would be genuine, with no intention to mislead. However, as inevitably occurs from time to time in most close relationships, tensions or quarrels will lead that woman to seek out her best friend – probably another woman – in order to gain sympathy and support. This ambivalence between partner and best friend has been nicely discussed in a recent essay by Kaeren Harrison on middle-class women. For them, friends were also those who 'were there for you' in times of need. They felt that they could be more 'authentic' with their friends: 'With your friends you just are.'

The relationship with the partner, however, has to be fitted into social and cultural expectations. Their initial commitments may have been made before the arrival of children or changing employment experiences have turned them into very different people. They may well have changed in different ways at different rates so that, in a very significant sense, they are no longer the same people who made the original commitments. Friends may help to confirm the fine-tuning of emerging identities.

It is frequently asserted that there is 'gender asymmetry in emotional expression' – a theme explored in depth in a series of essays by Jean Duncombe and Dennis Marsden. Men are often unwilling or unable to respond to their partner's needs. As one of Harrison's respondents put it:

> Well, my friend Rose is very intuitive. I could be telling the exact same story to my husband and he just wouldn't get it, you know? I mean, he would completely miss the point! But Rose would understand – I'd get a much better response from her. She'd give me good, considered advice. And I know that she would be really listening to me, and not just pretending to be listening from behind a newspaper.

Thus, for many middle-class women, while they may wish their partners to be their best friends, it is often their female friends who more closely meet their emotional needs. Kaeren Harrison suggests that, given the high incidence of divorce and single parenthood and some realistic pessimism about the longevity of marriage, it was a good, rational strategy for the women she investigated to develop close, personal relationships outside marriage.

Such women, even if they cannot name and do not have a close, communicative friendship of Aristotelian theory, at least know what they lack.

This is probably what lies behind the different approaches to friendship of Frankie Blue and Veronica in the novel. Lynn Jamieson has remarked in her book on *Intimacy* that 'friendships at the end of the century are a much more mixed bag in practice than the ideal of the "pure relationship", despite the pervasiveness of that ideal.' This is certainly true. Like Frankie and Veronica in the novel, social scientists can readily classify and codify people's friends – with or without the use of coloured pins. Seeing how these change through the life-course, as people move, split up and become more dependent through age or ill health, involves longitudinal or retrospective studies.

However, the codifying of friends does not necessarily tell us much about the contemporary role and meaning of friendship, how it may be changing and what generates these changes. Which social categories are likely to be friend-rich and which friend-poor? What are likely to be the social consequences if contemporary styles of friendship are able to suffuse kin links and the ties and obligation of kinship are suffusing friendship? One such consequence might be for the public support of carers to include certain friends as well as relatives.

It may be objected that the preceding discussion has implied that modern friendship is somehow the preserve of emotionally aware middle-class women, often with feminist sympathies. While traditional and classical sources focused on men's friendships, leaving women's friendships hidden, now the reverse may be the case. I return to this below in pages 122–30. A further objection might be that friendship among the working classes has been devalued, misunderstood or ignored.

The stereotype that emerged from some studies of working-class communities was that women lived in a world of family and kinship and men lived in the segregated worlds of pub, club and trade union. The close mother–daughter tie was of central and dominating importance, not paralleled by such a bonding between father and son or brothers. Men, it was argued, lacked the capacity to be articulate about feelings and emotions. They could go fishing together or gossip over innumerable pints of beer, but they were not into exploring the moral boundaries of their everyday life in the way it was claimed was achieved by the more loquacious and communicative women. In a study in the 1950s of what was described as 'a typical slum' in inner Liverpool, Madeline Kerr was able to claim: 'Occasionally individuals have personal friends but this is not very common in adult life.'

The middle class, by contrast, appeared to have the time, leisure, resources and social skills to accommodate friendship into their lives. Friends were useful in affirming and establishing social position, in providing suitable playmates for their children and in providing partners for various types of sport. In more intellectual and artistic circles, friendship was the basis of a form of self-indulgent fulfilment, as exemplified in the narcissistic writings of members of the Bloomsbury group. Most famously, perhaps, E. M. Forster, writing in the crisis year of 1939, shocked many contemporaries by saying:

> I hate the idea of causes, and if I had to choose between betraying my country and betraying my friends, I hope I should have the guts to betray my country . . . There lies at the back of every creed something terrible and hard for which the worshipper may one day be required to suffer, and there is even a terror and sadness in this creed of personal relationships, urbane and mild though it sounds.

Another Oxbridge don, C. S. Lewis, was even more explicit about the dangers of this approach to friendship. Writing in his book *The Four Loves*, published in 1960, he claimed that 'Every real friendship is a sort of secession, even a rebellion' which will generally be 'unwelcome to top people':

> Men who have real Friends are less easy to manage or 'get at', harder for good Authorities to correct or for bad Authorities to corrupt. Hence if our masters . . . ever succeed in producing a world where all are Companions and none are Friends, they will have removed certain dangers, and will also have taken from us what is almost our strongest safeguard against complete servitude.

This subversive type of friendship was widespread among the intelligentsia of former Communist Europe and the Soviet Union and contributed greatly to the various velvet revolutions in 1989.

However, this could be seen as a peculiarly Western, bourgeois view of friendship. Anthropologists have focused on the more instrumental aspects of friendship. When the anthropologist Julian Pitt-Rivers remarked that 'you can get nothing done in Andalucia save through friendship', he was referring not to the meeting of minds discussed by the Oxbridge dons but rather to a kind of lop-sided friendship which underlies systems of patronage. In an anthropological study of Sarakatsani shepherds in Greece in the 1960s, J. K. Campbell demonstrated how friendship is initiated and maintained by a continuing exchange of favours and goods, which are carefully accounted. The accumulation of friends can lead to more power, wealth and prestige – but at a cost. This instrumental view of friendship – Aristotle's friendship of utility

– has been rediscovered by sociologists in recent years, as we shall see below.

Is, then, friendship gender specific, class specific, context specific and so forth? Is it declining or increasing with modernity? Is contemporary friendship a shallow and fragmented way of shoring up our uncertain identities? Or is it the case, as some sociologists argue, that close, communicative friendship constitutes the highest and best quality in our personal relationships? These relationships are democratic and egalitarian: we choose them freely in a way not possible in the past. Perhaps a new intimacy is available to us as we enter the third millennium: men and women are learning to communicate together more deeply and in a more widespread manner than at any time in the past. Theodore Zeldin, in his book *An Intimate History of Humanity*, claims that while there were close and revealing friendships in the past they were typically between unusual people of the same gender. Now such close and enlarged forms of intimacy are available to a wider cross-section of the population.

Part of the problem, perhaps, is that those talking and writing about friendship are referring to very different social forms. Sociologists and social psychologists who attempt to quantify the importance and significance of friendship for different categories of the population at different stages of the life-course often have little knowledge of what it is, precisely, that they are measuring. The 'friend' for the slum dweller in Liverpool in the 1950s, for the Sarakatsani shepherds in mid-century Greece, or for Virginia Woolf and E. M. Forster are distinctively different.

It is clear that there is a world of difference between the friendship described in the philosophical writings of the Greeks and Romans, the rather pure and self-conscious soul-sharing of the medieval churchmen and the street-wise delusions of Frankie Blue. Friendship has to be seen in historical and cultural contexts. Some sociologists have been consistent in stressing this, while at the same time others have ignored it and have written about friendship in localized studies as if this had general validity for 'the working class', 'women' or whatever. In the next chapter we shall see how friendship changed in the eighteenth century to take its distinctive modern form and in Chapter 4 we shall consider in more detail how friendship changes through the life-course. In chapters 2 and 4 we draw more exclusively and extensively on the social science literature, but we return to more philosophical issues in Chapter 3.

2

Friendship, Modernity and Trust

> Friendship and the trust upon which it is based is
> thus a modern phenomenon, and decidedly not an
> aspect of premodern social formations.
>   Adam Seligman, *The Problem of Trust*

Much of sociology has been concerned with the understanding of 'modern' society, as it emerged from the eighteenth century Enlightenment, and has focused on the ensuing themes of industrialization, modernization, bureaucratization and secularization and similar clichés of student textbooks. The great bearded men who discussed the social disorganization of these momentous upheavals were generally pretty pessimistic: Karl Marx wrote of alienation and the class struggle, Max Weber referred to the burdens of the iron cage of bureaucracy and Émile Durkheim was concerned with moral disorder and the disintegration of social cohesion. Among other observers the diagnoses were no cheerier: de Tocqueville bemoaned the loss of the social solidarity and local democracy of small town America, while Sigmund Freud documented the neuroses of bourgeois Vienna and generalized widely about civilization and its discontents.

There appeared little likelihood that friendship would survive such momentous upheavals and intellectual onslaughts. The old comradely world of friends and neighbours of 'traditional society' was being replaced, so it was commonly asserted, by the anonymous competitive individualism of capitalist market society. One classic statement of this shift from *Gemeinschaft* to *Gesellschaft* – from community to association – was published by Ferdinand Tönnies in 1887. He saw social interaction in *gesellschaftlich* society as consisting:

> of an exchange of words and courtesies [in which] in reality everyone is thinking of himself in competition with the others. For everything pleasant which someone does for someone else, he expects, even demands, at least an equivalent. He weighs exactly his services, flatteries, presents, and so on, to determine whether they will bring about the desired result. Formless contracts are made continuously . . .

This style of thinking set the tone for much debate by sociologists for most of the twentieth century. In 1936 Dale Carnegie first published his enormously influential book *How to Win Friends and Influence People*. In the words of the American sociologists Robert Bellah and colleagues, in their rather doleful book on middle America entitled *Habits of the Heart* (1985), 'For Carnegie, friendship was an occupational tool for entrepreneurs, an instrument of the will in an inherently competitive society.' People with more friends are more likely to be emotionally adjusted: friends can help to achieve economic success and 'well-connected' people live longer, healthier lives. Getting more friends is, therefore, a matter of enlightened self-interest. However, as Bellah and colleagues point out, 'Are friends that one makes to improve one's health really friends enough to improve one's health?'

There is apparently plenty of evidence in the sociological literature that friends played a very minor part in most people's lives in the first part of the twentieth century. The classic study *Middletown* by Robert and Helen Lynd, published in 1929, set the tone for much that was to come. Of the 118 wives of working men in 'Middletown', forty had no friends or no intimate friends. These are some of the remarks that they make:

> It doesn't pay to be too friendly.

> Even your best friend will do you dirt. I never run around with people. I let everyone alone.

> Our neighbours used to be good friends and we had lots of good times together, but in the last seven or eight years all that's gone. People don't pay much attention to each other any more.

> I don't even know the names of the people next door and we have lived here a year.

> I have no intimate friends; it is difficult and too involving to become intimate with anybody but a few close relatives.

The working-class women in Middletown all agreed that times had changed:

> We ain't got neighbours any more. People ain't so friendly as they used to be. There's less neighbourhood visiting.

Those whom the Lynds call 'women of the business class' were more ready to welcome this trend towards privatization: 'I like this way of living in a neighbourhood where you can be friendly with people but not intimate and dependent.' Many are quoted as saying that people no longer call on each other in Middletown. Whether this was due to the uncertainties brought on by the looming economic depression, or whether those who are engaged on a trajectory of social mobility and are seeking success need to travel light, is hard to say. Whatever the cause, mid-century sociologists were much impressed by the apparent social isolation induced by competitive and possessive individualism.

Another community study, *Crestwood Heights*, actually a suburb of Toronto, was published in 1956 and fitted in well with the thesis developed in *The Lonely Crowd, Abundance for What?* and similar pessimistic writings of David Riesman and others. However, in fairness, Riesman did acknowledge that 'it is hard for description not to become parody when we are reading not about strata or tribes remote from us, but about our own suburban life.' Mid-century suburban North America was the *locus classicus* of male careerism and sharply segregated gender roles, with 'the mother' and 'the wife' trapped in the little boxes on the hillside (all looking the same) and suffering, in Betty Friedan's phrase, from 'the disease that has no name'. Returning home from the instrumental corporate world, 'Crestwood Man' would 'rarely . . . come wholeheartedly to endorse the democratic and permissive norms now seeping into the family'. Patriarchy ruled. This is how the authors characterize the tragedy of suburban North America in mid-century:

> Social mobility demands . . . that the people of Crestwood Heights experience, in the span from physical birth to physical death, a series of minor psychic deaths. Fathers, mothers, brothers, sisters, kin, friends and neighbours are all seen as necessarily expendable. But this necessity, in all its starkness, also holds out the promise of rebirth, not once, not twice, but many times during the course of one natural life.

Social and geographical mobility driven by the overwhelming desire for material success was seen to be
undermining the American character: the loss of friends
and friendship was simply part of a larger and socially
damaging process. Philip Slater's book *The Pursuit of
Loneliness* (1970) was subtitled 'American Culture at the
Breaking Point'.

While many intellectuals and critics wrote perceptively
about the dehumanizing consequences of mass society in
mid-century America, sociologists, perhaps with a mis-
placed attempt to be professional and rigorous, came to
approach friends, particularly friends of utility, and friend-
like relations in terms of economic analogies. Exchange
theory, as it came to be called, theorized and legitimated
the writings of Dale Carnegie and the individualistic competitive drive for success. Peter Blau's book *Exchange and
Power in Social Life* was published in 1964 and George
Homans's *Social Behaviour: Its Elementary Forms* came out
three years earlier. While these books differ in certain
significant ways, they both argue that individuals associate
with one another fundamentally because they all gain
profit from their associations.

The humane and subtle insights of Aristotle and Cicero
are reformulated by Peter Blau in terms of exchange
theory. For human beings to establish social associations
on their own initiative (i.e. make friends) they have to be
induced by the force of social attraction: 'An individual is
attracted to another if he expects associating with him to
be in some way rewarding for himself, and his interest in
the expected social rewards draws him to the other.' Both
parties have to anticipate that the association will be
rewarding, and this is the basis of the attraction underlying
the association. Following this mutual attraction, people
will form an association and will start rewarding each
other. Unless their expectations are disappointed their

association will continue, based on their mutual attractions: 'Processes of social attraction, therefore, lead to processes of social exchange.' Exchange processes, argues Blau, give rise to a differentiation of power.

George Homans similarly develops some general propositions which envisage social behaviour as 'an exchange of activity, tangible or intangible and more or less rewarding or costly between at least two persons'. Homans draws on other research which shows, unsurprisingly, that friends interacted more often than non-friends. Friends are more likely to have rewarded each other in the past and so there will be an incentive to interact again, providing an opportunity for more rewards. A person who is not a friend does not present the same stimulus and may not therefore be given an opportunity to show how rewarding he might be.

Homans's behaviourist approach owes much to the experimental psychological behaviourist B. F. Skinner. Blau, on the other hand, introduces his section on basic processes with a quotation from Adam Smith's work *The Theory of Moral Sentiments*, first published in 1761, emphasizing that to reward is to return good for good and to punish is to return evil for evil.

Reading these and other mid-twentieth-century theorists, one could readily come to the conclusion that modern social theory was recognizing and indeed accepting the inevitable commodification of social relationships. In order to acquire friends it seemed to be necessary to impress others with the anticipation of rewards. Erving Goffman, in his many books on the importance of impression management, was another who adopted this highly utilitarian approach. The assumption appeared to be that people were slippery little tricksters endlessly engaged in games of one-upmanship with each other.

Furthermore, while it was not explicit in the writings of

Blau, Goffman and others, many other commentators of the period argued that it was not always thus. The calculative attitudes of mid-century American people were brought about by new insecurities based on a fluctuating social scene. Upwardly mobile people were reluctant to put down strong roots since that would be likely to make the regular transplanting to new locales more difficult. Drawing on studies such as those of Middletown or Crestwood Heights already mentioned, it was argued that this was an inevitable result of modernity. Whereas in traditional society friends and neighbours provided secure support, in 'the modern world' there is a 'breakdown of community' in the interests of the 'free mobility of labour'.

These and similar arguments rest on two main assumptions: first, that warm affective relationships with non-kin were characteristic of 'traditional' society and, second, that the writings of Adam Smith and others in the period of the eighteenth-century Enlightenment ushered in a new, modern approach to social relationships, based on market rationality.

The transformation of friendship in the eighteenth century

The reconstruction of past mentalities is a notoriously difficult exercise given the inevitably scanty evidence. However, the distinguished historian Lawrence Stone has concluded:

> Such personal correspondence and diaries as survive suggest that social relations from the fifteenth to the seventeenth centuries tended to be cool, even unfriendly. The extraordinary amount of casual inter-personal physical and verbal violence, as recorded in legal and other records,

shows clearly that at all levels men and women were
extremely short-tempered. . . . Friends and acquaintances
felt honour bound to challenge and kill others for the
slightest affront, however unintentional or spoken in the
careless heat of passion or drink.

Stone claimed that, even in 'traditional village communities', expressions of hatred reached levels of frequency,
intensity and duration that are rarely matched today
(apart, he suggests, from that found among close-knit
groups such as fellows of Oxbridge colleges!). Stone also
suggests that in medieval England homicide was much
more likely to be outside the family than within it. The
family was more a unit for the perpetration of crime than
a focus for it. As he memorably put it 'the family that
slayed together, stayed together.' The emotional ties
between family members appeared to be weaker than the
strong feelings that led to intra-familial murder. 'Alienation and distrust of one's fellow men are the predominant
features of the Elizabethan and early Stuart view of human
character and conduct.' He cites a 'Letter of Advice to a
Son' – a common form of literary and moral exercise
among the landed classes – namely that by Sir William
Wentworth to his son, the future Earl of Stafford, written
in 1607. His basic assumption is that no one is to be
trusted – with the possible exception of his wife or 'a
private faithful friend'. Sir William suggests: 'He that will
be honoured and feared in his country must bear counten-
ance and authority, for people are servile, not generous,
and do reverence men for fear, not for love of their
virtues.' This highly cynical view of the nature of social
relationships, which included wives and kin as well as
friends, is likely to be general where there is not a well-
established and secure civil society.

Before the eighteenth century the phrase 'my friends'

meant little more than 'my advisors, associates and backers' and would be likely to include relatives, neighbours or persons of higher status from whom one might expect patronage. 'Friends' were likely to be important advisors in connection with marriage for those from the lower middle class to the highest social levels. These 'friends' – always in the plural – meant a collection of parents, guardians, old uncles and so on, and the term used in this sense persisted well into the nineteenth century. For Sir William Wentworth, these elderly family associates would not necessarily have any specific ties of affection for his son, and he referred to them in much the same way that a father might now recommend a reliable accountant or stockbroker.

At the village level, according to Stone, there was little warmth and tolerance in interpersonal relations. They were places filled with malice and hatred: 'What is being postulated for the sixteenth and early seventeenth centuries is a society in which a majority of the individuals that composed it found it very difficult to establish close emotional ties to any other person . . . adults treated each other with suspicion and hostility; affect was low and hard to find . . . So far as the surviving evidence goes, England between 1500 and 1660 was relatively cold, suspicious and violence prone.' However, by the mid-eighteenth century a highly significant change seems to have taken place. The word 'friend' comes to have its modern (and original) meaning. Dr Johnson's *Dictionary* defined it as 'one who supports you and comforts you while others do not' and as someone 'with whom to compare minds and cherish private virtues'.

So how did this change take place? Far from traditional society being suffused with brotherly *gemeinschaftlich* virtues, the reverse appears to be the case. Counter to what the classical sociological tradition appears to suggest, Aris-

totelian styles of friendship re-emerged with the coming
of commercial-industrial society in the eighteenth century.
This seems to turn conventional wisdom on its head.
Those who argue for the commodification of social
relationships, a retreat to a privatized home world and the
growth of a new rational calculus, seeing social cohesion
in terms of analogies with economic theories of exchange,
have perhaps been more prone to assertion than to a
careful consideration of the evidence.

A casual reader of exchange theorists such as Peter Blau
might be forgiven for assuming that Adam Smith had a
predominantly market-oriented view of society, which suffused all social forms. However, in a highly stimulating
and original paper, the American sociologist Allan Silver
has provided a radical reassessment of friendship in the
emerging commercial society. He points out that Adam
Smith actually rejected a model of exchange theory, drawn
from the impersonal market, as being applicable to personal relations. Silver stoutly claims that 'The father of
market theory was precisely not an "exchange theorist" in
the domain of personal relationships.'

Paradoxically, and counter to what is assumed in much
modern social theory, it was precisely the spread of market
exchange in the eighteenth century that led to the development of new benevolent bonds. The particularistic basis
of earlier commercial reciprocities did not fit in well with
the new rational-legal bureaucratic society that was emerging. The eighteenth-century philosophers of the Enlightenment recognized that personal moralities, far from being
a mere reflection of commercial exigencies, had their own
separate and distinctive basis, which could not easily be
accommodated to the newly emerging formal codes.
Adam Smith, in *The Theory of Moral Sentiments*, recognized the distinctiveness and formlessness of personal
relations in commercial society. There are no clear rules,

he suggested, to determine precisely the nature of friendship, and so obviously it is not at all possible to behave strictly in accordance with some pre-existing formula. 'The actions required by friendship, humanity, hospitality, generosity are', Smith insisted, 'vague and indeterminate.'

The notion that there should be some way of measuring a 'norm of reciprocity' struck Adam Smith as being ludicrous. Any rule to determine what and how one should repay a particular service would 'admit of a thousand exceptions'.

> If your friend lent you money in your distress, ought you to lend him some in his? How much ought you lend him? When ought you lend him? Now, or tomorrow, or next month? And for how long a time? It is evident that no general rule can be laid down, by which a precise answer can, in all cases, be given to any of these questions. The difference between his character and yours, between his circumstances and yours, may be such, that you may be perfectly grateful, and justly refuse to lend him a half-penny; on the contrary, you may be willing to lend him ten times the sum which he lent you and yet be justly accused of the blackest ingratitude, and of not having fulfilled the hundredth part of the obligation you lie under.

Quite clearly, Adam Smith rejected any economistic model or an analogy between market exchange and the personal relations of friendship. Sometime in the eighteenth century, it seems, friendship appeared as one of a new set of benevolent social bonds. This was not as some kind of sharp reaction to the dehumanizing aspects of commercial society but rather as an essential moral and psychological ingredient of new liberal and fraternal values. Allan Silver quotes very appropriately from Rousseau's *Emile* to make the point:

The only bond of my associations would be mutual attachment, agreement of tastes, suitableness of characters . . . I
would want to have a society around me, not a court;
friends and not *protégés*. I would not be the patron of any
guests; I would be their host. The independence and
equality would permit my relationships to have all the
candour of benevolence; and where neither duty nor
interest entered in any way, pleasure and friendship would
alone make the law.

Allan Silver argues convincingly that the paradigmatic
shift in the nature and meaning of friendship which was
associated with the growth of commercial society was
better understood by the social theorists of the eighteenth
century than by the theories of Marx, Tönnies or Sir
Henry Maine, whom he categorizes as 'often derivative,
reactive or sentimental'. Unfortunately, it is these same
reactive and sentimental theories that have done so much
to influence modern sociology in general and the theoretical understanding of friendship in particular. It is from
the more sure foundation of the eighteenth-century moral
philosophers that we can move on to consider some of the
essential   sociological   ingredients   of   contemporary
friendship.

In his *Treatise of Human Nature* (1739–40) David Hume
celebrated the moral quality of friendship:

It is remarkable that nothing touches a man of humanity
more than any instance of extraordinary delicacy in love or
friendship, where a person is attentive to the smallest
concerns of his friend, and is willing to sacrifice to them
the most considerable interest of his own.

The crucial point is that David Hume, Adam Smith,
Adam Ferguson and others were rejoicing in the *liberation*
of friendship from the narrow instrumental concerns of

pre-commercial society as described by Lawrence Stone. The replacement of much previous instrumental friendship by the rules of commercial society allowed the free expression of a new morally superior friendship based on 'natural sympathy' unconstrained by necessity. These new, freely chosen relationships reflected the new universalism emerging in civil society. The well-regulated market frees the classic Aristotelian friendship of virtue from friendship of utility. Commercial society requires 'authentically indifferent co-citizens' rather than potential enemies or allies.

Nevertheless, for the newly urbanized workers in a rapidly expanding capitalism there appeared to be many social forces preventing the spread of these new forms of friendly relations. The American social theorists of the Chicago School writing in the 1920s emphasized the transience and impermanence of urban life, following the suggestions of Georg Simmel, who in his essay *The Metropolis and Mental Life* first published in *Die Grosstadt* in 1902–3, wrote of the reserve and distrust which men have in 'the touch-and-go elements of metropolitan life'. Simmel influenced very heavily the approach of the Chicago ethnographers, particularly through the work of Robert Park and Louis Wirth. Perhaps overdeterministically, Simmel claimed that 'the quantitative aspect of life is transformed *directly* into qualitative traits of character' (my italics). Urban life transformed the traditional struggle with nature into an inter-human struggle for gain. The division of labour leads to narrow one-sidedness and 'death to the personality of the individual'. In his major treatise *The Philosophy of Money* (1900) he reiterates the point about commodification of personal relationships thus:

> Money results in a universal objectification of transactions, in an elimination of all personal nuances and tendencies,

and, further, that the number of relationships based on money is constantly increasing, that the significance of one person for another can increasingly be traced back, even though often in a concealed form, to monetary interests. In this way, an inner barrier develops between people, a barrier, however, that is indispensable for the modern form of life . . . sensitive and nervous modern people would sink completely into despair if the objectification of social relationships did not bring with it an inner boundary and reserve.

This is an interpretation that is in direct contrast with that of Adam Smith who considered that the existence of numerous indifferent strangers was more likely to help define the moral order rather than weaken it. The 'strangers' of commercial society are not friends who can offer special favours or sympathies; but similarly they are not our enemies from whom we can expect no sympathy. Since the particularistic and exclusivist bonds defined by custom, corporate group and so on are dissolved, a new sympathy moderates ideas and conducts, distributing fellow-feeling in an essentially democratic spirit. Before commercial society a main purpose of friendship was to help friends by deflecting enemies, whereas in the eighteenth century personal relations benefited those involved at no cost to others. As Allan Silver remarks, this implied that 'friendship becomes simultaneously a private virtue and a public good.'

So Adam Smith, Adam Ferguson and others recognized that the great virtue of commercial society was to allow a clear distinction to be made between those relationships based on interest and those relationships based on sympathy and affection. Before this clear distinction emerged, people were advised to treat friends as if they might become enemies. Hence, in commercial society the family may be weakened and friendship strengthened, as Adam Smith explains:

> In commercial countries, where the authority of law is always perfectly sufficient to protect the meanest man in the state . . . [families], having no . . . motive for keeping together naturally separate or disperse as interest or inclination may direct.

Social mobility is likely to reduce friend-like relations to develop between those kin who find themselves at different positions in the social hierarchy. Friendship is more likely to be characteristic of the conjugal relationship. Francis Hutcheson, in his *System of Moral Philosophy* (1755), remarks:

> Nature has designed the conjugal state to be a constant reciprocal friendship of two . . . the tender sentiments and affections which engage the parties into this relation of marriage, plainly declare it to be a state of equal partnership or friendship, and not such a one wherein the one party stipulates to himself a right of governing in all domestick affairs, and the other promises subjection.

Over 240 years later Anthony Giddens, in his book *The Transformation of Intimacy*, argued for the emergence of confluent relationships in very similar terms. However, in fairness to Giddens, the Scottish liberals were not as progressive as they might seem, since they assumed that, in practice, wives would voluntarily cede many of their theoretical rights to their husbands. However, the Scots did claim that it is only in commercial society that friendship can connect. In the words of Allan Silver, 'Only with impersonal markets in products and services does a parallel system of personal relations emerge whose ethic

excludes exchange and utility.' Friendship and other sympathetic bonds serve to integrate individuals into the larger
society. This is a theme well developed in modern sociology to which we shall return in Chapter 5.

However, Silver is highly critical of much contemporary
sociology of personal relations for exhibiting a naive 'presentism' associated with the lack of historical understanding. Hence, when sociologists 'rediscovered' primary
relations in modern society, they mistakenly assumed that
there were survivals of what had been an essential feature
of traditional society. Admittedly, much of the relevant
social history has become available only in the last thirty
or forty years but it is undoubtedly the case that the
notion of a pre-industrial 'traditional' society was uncriti-
cally assumed as a stereotype, and sociologists overlooked
the pre-Comptean liberal thinkers of the eighteenth
century.

Any attempt to pluck 'community' and personal relations out of specific contexts is an exercise fraught with
difficulties and pitfalls. Any suggestion that there have
been qualitative or quantitative changes in the texture and
style of relationships must assume that it is possible to
compare like with like. However, different social structures, cultures and contexts cannot be put on a continuum
in such a way. As Silver aptly asks:

> Are the intense loyalties, coexisting with the frank expec-
> tation of reward, found in codes and cultures of honour
> before commercial society, the same 'conceptual stuff' as
> the loyalties of modern friends and the instrumentalism of
> market society? Or are the sense, setting and substance of
> 'honour' so different that 'differentiation' smuggles the
> present into the past and suppresses questions that might
> otherwise be asked, both about past and present? How
> much of our view of the transformation of personal rela-

tions by markets and bureaucracies is created artificially by the tendentiousness of our tools?

But we must not make the same mistake by applying the analysis of the Scots in the eighteenth century to the contemporary world. The Scots were analysing commercial not capitalist society, their moral theory was addressed to modestly Christian merchant gentlemen, and their vision of sociability and civic virtue was formed in the ideologies of the times. Nor must we make the same mistake with the nineteenth-century romantics trapped in their anti-capitalist critiques. Sociologists need to be aware of the historical and intellectual context in which each theoretical paradigm develops. The idea of placing friendship in context is a current theoretical challenge. No longer can the sociological presentism of much contemporary writing about men's or women's friendship or the imputed distinctions between 'middle-class' and 'working-class' friendship patterns be discussed without recognizing the distinctiveness of the social, political and economic circumstances of the time.

Friendship and trust

There is an emerging modern ideal of friendship. This is not based on rules, regulations or any part of the institutionalized order. Individuals, out of their own volition, work out how they should behave with their friends. At the heart of this ideal is the notion of trust. It is axiomatic that friends should not betray each other, and hence personal trust has a moral quality, although there may be limits on how far friends should support those who do transcend the moral boundaries of their particular social worlds. Grassing on one's mates is not done. But should one tell the social services if one believes that a friend is abusing her child? In his very useful report *Friendship Networks and Social Support,* carried out in North London in the mid-1980s, Peter Willmott quotes one of his respondents, a working-class man, as saying: 'I stop being friends with someone if he starts trying to get off with my wife.' Quite evidently, such a friendship is not based on trust.

Allan Silver has successfully encapsulated in one of his essays the modern ideal of friendship. He agrees with C. S. Lewis, E. M. Forster (quoted above) and many others who argue that friendship in its highest form must invert the forms of association and the ways of the larger society.

> In this ideal, friendships are voluntary, unspecialised, informal and private . . . Friendships are diminished in moral quality if terms of exchange between friends are consciously or scrupulously monitored, for this implies that utilities derived from friendships are constitutive as in market relations, rather than valued as expressions of personal intentions and commitments.

Friendship can produce deep, enduring and binding attachments completely free from any form or body of legal or administrative regulation. If we feel obliged to be a friend, then it is no true friendship. In the modern ideal of friendship, the relationship is one of our own free choosing, it is a product of our own personal agency and no other. We create and keep our friendships by conscious acts of will. In Samuel Johnson's words, 'A man, Sir, should keep his friendships in constant repair.'

This vision of the modern ideal of friendship is related to the late modern concern – if not obsession – with individual freedom and expression. Those who commit themselves to this ideal and desire to acquire, as it were, another self must thereby expose their vulnerability. The inevitable uncertainties of interpersonal interactions have to be overcome through trust. This implies that trust must lie at the heart of true communicative friendship in the contemporary world. There are no rules and contracts to bind us to our closest friends: we simply have to trust them. The closer we are to our friends, the more able they are to betray us. Without trust, friendships will fail. Immanuel Kant, while recognizing the importance of true friendship, remarked that if one person 'reveals his failings while the other person concealed his own, he would lose something of the other's respect by presenting himself so candidly.'

We have to behave as if our friend will not betray us, even though we recognize that she has the capacity to do so. Our personal trust has to transcend this possibility: unlike formal contracts or activities enforceable by third parties, this trust is based on a moral quality. Allan Silver puts this in formal sociological terms:

> Trust takes on a moral urgency because it affirms the impossibility of betrayal despite its existential possibility ... Friendship in modern culture is morally celebrated, in part, as a pure expression in the domain of personal relations of voluntary agency, as expressing individual agency and elective interpersonal affinities that in principle, if not in fact, are independent of ascriptive and categorical criteria.

Silver goes on to argue very persuasively that it is ahistorical to impose these aspects of a modern ideal of friendship on to the past and on to other societies. This is very easily done, and I fear that this book is no exception: there are instances when I refer to the Aristotelian pure form of friendship of virtue as if it can be transposed without qualification to contemporary society. Strictly this cannot be done, since the social form of friendship must be related to the encapsulating social formation of the society as a whole. We live in a capitalist society, not a slave society or a feudal society. This will unquestionably affect the way we develop the personal, which may be more or less constricted by wider structures and processes.

Allan Silver believes that modern friendship is 'proto-typically the most 'personal' relationship possible', whereas Simmel fears that we have 'too much to hide to sustain a friendship in the ancient sense'. He believed that, apart from, perhaps, in one's earliest years, we are 'too uniquely individualised to allow full reciprocity of understanding and reciprocity'. On balance, as the rest of the book will reveal, I lean towards Silver's view, although, following La Rochefoucauld, I would feel that 'However rare true love may be, it is less so than true friendship.'

This reliance on feelings may seem an odd position for a sociologist to hold. Surely there must be ways of measuring this problematical 'true friendship' empirically so that a precise answer can be given. Those who have attempted to measure 'true' or 'real' friends, such as the sociologists Graham Allan or Peter Willmott, unsurprisingly come back to the question of trust. So are we becoming more or less able to trust one another?

What is it about a specific social formation that helps or hinders the development of trust in the personal sphere? There have been a number of serious attempts to come to grips with this problem in recent years, and there does seem to be an emerging consensus that its existence is greater (or perhaps the need of it is greater) in modern social formations. But because it seems so difficult to understand the nature of trust, it becomes equally difficult to understand the prevalence of 'real' friendship. One of the early contributors to the debate, James Coleman, in his *Foundations of Social Theory*, posed a question that was by no means simple, namely, 'Why are persons slow to trust a friend and quick to trust a confidence man?' Trust can be maintained in a close community with many norms and sanctions to support it. But what leads to a social environment where men and women can come to trust each other intimately as close friends? In his stimulating essay provocatively entitled 'Can We Trust Trust?' Diego Gambetta argues persuasively that it may be rational to trust trust and distrust distrust. In a curious way he provides a rational justification for the necessity of accepting a self-fulfilling prophecy: 'The concession of trust . . . can generate the very behaviour which might logically seem to be its pre-condition.'

However, awkwardly, we still do not know what trust is, other than some kind of belief in the good will of the other. But what is the nature of this belief? Furthermore, if people are more trusting in certain contexts or societies than in others, does this mean that the capacity and potential for developing true friendship is equally variable? Do children grow up more securely and trustingly in some social environments than in others? If they are too trusting, are they more likely to be duped by con-men than to form deep and enduring friendships?

Since this is a complex topic, central to an important current debate in sociology, this is not an appropriate place to make a comprehensive review of the issues. Anthony Giddens recognizes that trust must imply non-rational and incalculable elements, implying that it is a form of faith in which 'confidence vested in probable outcomes expresses a commitment to something rather than just a cognitive understanding.' But clearly this is only part of it. There is a distinction between trust – where, for example, an individual has to take a risk to make a decision to trust one colleague rather than another

– and confidence – where one has a general expectation that a particular colleague will carry out his teaching responsibilities regularly and effectively. 'What makes trust so puzzling', remarks Barbara Misztal, 'is that to trust involves more than believing; in fact trust is to believe despite uncertainty. Trust always involves an element of risk resulting from our inability to monitor others' behaviour, from our inability to have a complete knowledge about other people's motivations and, generally, from the contingency of social reality.'

It is strange that political and social theorists have not seen the need to explore the nature of trust empirically by focusing on the deepest and closest forms of friendship. Arguably, this is the *locus classicus* for the exploration of trust in contemporary society, since social relations and the obligations inherent in them are mainly responsible for the production of trust. Intimacy is a strategy of establishing trust. Allan Silver claims that friendship bonds in the modern world are potentially limitless. They are free from any constraints of institutional context and are morally bounded only by our capacities to meet them. Evidently, the better the friend, the closer the bond and the less defined or limited the potential demands. This open-ended form of friendship is distinctively modern, but it does have strong echoes of Aristotle's conception of another self. However, there may be some connotations in Chapter 1 (and again in the chapters that follow) that this pure, trusting, communicative friendship is based on some kind of intellectual meeting of minds. There may be an unwarranted intellectual arrogance in the suggestion that the higher-educated, self-consciously reflexive colonizers of post-modernity are exploring something that ordinary people cannot experience or achieve. There is a further danger that a disciplined and intellectual dissection of the nature of trust may unwittingly allow the essence of friendships of virtue to melt under the heat of scrutiny.

In order to counter any such false and misleading impressions, I reproduce what one working-class woman in Peter Willmott's survey told him. This is not an isolated example. There are many varied statements in contemporary ethnographies of ordinary working women, often presented by other women anxious to provide a voice for those who are generally unheard. The important point that comes out clearly in what follows is that women reciprocally *sense* the intimate closeness and trust of their friendship.

A close friend is someone who doesn't have to be told when you are in trouble. They sense it. They don't need to ask if the children are ill. If they come round and see that one of the children looks a bit poorly, they immediately offer to help. Or if something is worrying me, my friend Marion (living nearby) just senses it. I don't have to ask. She'll say 'I can see you're upset about something. You just sit down and I'll get on with whatever it is'. And the same with her. If she's upset or worrying about something, I can sense it.

3

Friendship and the Self

Better a true friend than a relation.

Old Turkish proverb

Friendship is a serious affection; the most sublime of all affections because it is founded on principle, and cemented by time. The very reverse may be said of love. In a great degree, love and friendship cannot subsist in the same bosom; even when inspired by different objects, they weaken or destroy each other, and for the same object can only be felt in succession.

Mary Wollstonecraft
A Vindication of the Rights of Women

To keep friendship in proper order, the balance of good offices must be preserved, otherwise a disquieting and anxious feeling creeps in, and destroys mutual comfort.

Charlotte Brontë

As we saw in Chapter 1, the great ages of friendship could be claimed to be in the past – the classical world of Aristotle and Cicero and the early Christian church – or possibly the bohemian world of the Bloomsbury group or similar coteries. According to this view, the present age is one of great superficiality, of networking and filofaxing, of contrived forename mateyness at work and of gushy 'luv-vies' calling each other darling. The socialite with 'hun-dreds of friends' has no friends: she simply has many refractions of an ever-changing kaleidoscopic self with no centre. Such 'friends' disappear when the patronage or social advantages decline.

Yet the counter-view that friendship is reaching new levels of depth and complexity in the modern world is more persuasive. In the classical writings on friendship, the truly great 'friendships of virtue' could apparently exist only between men of good character. Classical authors imply that women at that time were insufficiently edu-cated or developed in their sensibilities or too oppressed by men to be in a position to develop close, character-forming friendships. Friendships between men and women were, therefore, singularly rare and problematic. In the modern, contemporary world, however, with increasing social and geographical mobility, friendship, it is argued, has at last come into its own. No longer the preserve of a privileged male elite, it is suffusing kin and family relationships as never before. Women rely on other women to affirm their identities, often in the face of criticism from parents unable to cope with feminist or non-mainstream heterosexual gender roles. Men have similar problems as they move to more non-traditional roles and wish to explore their feelings as fathers or as gays with other men. Parents die, children leave home, couples dissolve and reunite; the emotional traumas of contemporary life take place in different places with differ-ent key actors. Sometimes the only continuity for increas-ingly reflexive people is provided by their friends. Unwilling to be perceived as social chameleons flitting from one job or partner to another, men and women may come to rely on their friends to provide support and confirmation of their enduring identities.

Furthermore, close friends may provide the necessary guidance and support for our rather muddled desire to be decent or good. How should we live in a way that in our hearts we find morally acceptable? The answer is provided by the guidance, support and example of our friends. If they knew what we are doing would they approve? Can I expect him or her to be my friend if I do not do this or that? We explore loyalty, trust and betrayal in our dealings with our friends. Our friends have the potential to shame us, but friendship cannot be based on fear. So we have to be prepared to show weakness in order to confirm that we trust our friends.

Perhaps it may help at this point to introduce an empirical example to illustrate how one particular articulate and reflexive young woman manages her friends. She may be seen as typical of a new generation of university-educated professional young women striving to forge a contemporary identity. Not all young women in her situation would be so single-minded in the care and effort she deploys to hold her circle of friends together.

Sue is a woman of thirty-five with a personal community of 'best friends' which she has gradually accumulated, beginning at her primary school. She added others at secondary school, sixth-form college and university and acquired a cluster after her second job. The mother of one of her female friends became her mentor and supported her as she struggled with her emotional development in her twenties. Her sister – now more than a sister – a friend and soul-mate, carried her daily letters to her friend at another primary school. Later, when Sue had a child with her current partner, she was able to see her sister and her partner as the firm social rocks of her world. Beyond this core are her circles of 'best' and 'close' friends, with whom she works very hard to maintain contact and continuity. Hour-long talks on the telephone, regular visits at weekends – often driving hundreds of miles on the round trips – and lengthy letters are all necessary to keep her social support group active. She sometimes goes off for weekend holidays with three other women whom she met at work. They have a regular commitment to spending a night together in each other's houses in turn. Sue talks of her distinctive style of managing her friends, recognizing that others manage their friends differently. She can cope with only seven or eight but these are crucially important for her and provided continuity and support for her changing identity as she moved through education, training and employment to motherhood.

As a young mother Sue needs the support of other young mothers living nearby whom she can turn to for advice and help in day-to-day crises. She says that she would not yet class these as part of her personal community. However, one of them is shaping up well and she accepts the possibility that, if they get to know each other better, she may make the transition to 'close' friend.

These young women are bound together through talk: they pour out their innermost feelings to each other about their jobs, relationships, partners and children. They are working out together who they are and what their emerging identities might be in a fluid world of social and geographical mobility. Sue mentions in passing that one of her friends is black, another had been a secretary at Sue's place of work but is now living with a car salesman and another is a lesbian. Differences in class, age, ethnicity and sexual orientation can be easily accommodated in Sue's personal community. The most unusual friend is possibly the woman who acted as her mentor, Lorraine, who is a psychologist and is now over sixty years old. At times she seems to have served as an unpaid therapist to Sue, who has perhaps made a hobby of reflexivity. Lorraine's relationship with Sue has changed for the worse,

Sue hints, since her son, a scientist, is now Sue's partner. She did not meet him until long after her friendship with his mother was established. The easy basis of their friendship is being suffused with quasi-kinship obligations and expectations. Lorraine is taking an understandable interest and pleasure in being a grandmother and this introduces different dimensions, where age and status gain a new salience. Since Sue and her partner are now thinking of getting married, affinal kinship roles are likely to get stronger. Sue will then try to encourage 'friend-like' relationships to suffuse her new kin links.

Since Sue works so hard in maintaining her personal community and, as she says, she could not imagine existing without it, how could it ever change? The common bonds of shared experience make it a kind of 'family of choice', albeit largely of the same age range, though not homogeneous in many other social respects. We would have to follow this personal community as it grows or declines through Sue's life. This is what I have referred to as her social convoy. Some people have what I call 'fossil friends', who were particularly important at one stage of life – perhaps at university for example – but who move away and are not part of an individual's active personal community. However, if circumstances happen to change, the 'fossil friend' may be reactivated and the friendship would carry on 'just where it left off'.

Sue had no fossil friends but she had consciously dropped one friend and was in danger of losing another. In the case of the first, it appeared that, despite being very close, this friend had racist views which had remained undisclosed for a long time. Since friendship for Sue was about morality, integrity and the sort of person she wants to see herself as being, the friendship had to end. Another friendship is at risk because the woman in question has married 'successfully' and is moving in circles and entertaining at a level which Sue cannot match. She is coming to feel socially ill at ease in her friend's new circle. However much she cares for her friend she feels she is drawing apart from her.

The importance of communication and talk is central. Sue needs friends less for practical support, although her less-close friends locally do provide this. She distinguishes between her 'best' friends and 'close' friends in terms of their moral qualities and emotional capacities. Friendship for her is part of a highly personal inner journey: it is part of the good life.

Friendship is treated in a rather cavalier way in most social surveys: respondents are frequently asked how many friends they have, how often they see them, how far away they are, whether they are of the same social status and so on. Sometimes social networks are constructed to show the interlinkages between the various social atoms designated as friends. Classifications are typically of the crudest kind, and very rarely are respondents asked what they mean when they use the word 'friend'. In many analyses sharp distinctions are made between family and kinship and friends, recognizing that the agnatic and affinal ties are enduring and that their rights, duties and responsibilities are commonly understood and may have the backing of family law to support them. Friends, by contrast, while claimed to be a significant part of social life, are seen as the accessories rather than the basic garments that surround one's social self. They are freely chosen and the moral obligations that they may carry are less binding and important than those relating to basic kin ties such as those between parents and children. Such is a commonly held view.

However, when Sue was telling me of the relative closeness of members of her personal community, while her sister was in the innermost circle, her brother was at the edge. And this wasn't simply a matter of gender: in the case of other respondents in our Essex University research project, it was the other way round, with dominant or competitive sisters placed at the periphery of the personal community. Sue felt obliged to put her parents closer in on her map of social distance – not because she was particularly close to them but because she recognized the social expectation that parents and children ought to be close, with the only socially legitimate category as an acceptable intrusion between them being her partner and their children. She recognized that in reality she was much closer to some of her friends – particularly her mentor Lorraine – than she was to her parents, but her model of 'kinship in the mind' was that parents 'ought' to be more significant than friends.

There is now increasing sociological evidence from the work of, for example, Janet Finch and Jennifer Mason on conventional families and Jeffrey Weeks on the gay community that the notion that kinship must, inevitably, be at the core of people's personal communities should be questioned. Some family members are more congenial and 'friend-like' than others. People are claiming more choice in deciding with which, if any, family members they want to remain in close contact. Those family and kin with whom they closely interact are becoming more 'friend-like'. Perhaps, reciprocally, those friends with whom they get on most closely are becoming more 'kin-like': many friends of those dying of AIDS, for example, have found themselves in the 'next-of-kin' role. Similarly, in the case of partners, it is increasingly the case that it is not the traditional 'wifely' or 'husbandly' qualities that are most sought after but rather the qualities of a good friend: being tolerant, supportive, humorous, companionable, engaging in common interests, having strong intuitive insight and so forth.

But if the meaning and significance of friends and friendship is changing in our society, how can surveys asking precise questions about numbers and frequencies report accurately on social reality? Maybe people themselves are confused and refer to different styles and qualities of relationships. The word 'friend' covers a broad continuum of possible forms and styles of relationships.

As we saw in Chapter 1, Georg Simmel writing a century ago, claimed that whole-hearted soul-mates are more difficult to establish in modern society – except, perhaps, in marriage. 'The modern way of feeling tends more heavily toward differentiated friendships, which cover only one side of the personality, without playing into other aspects of it', he wrote. Thus, according to this view, we play tennis with one friend, watch football with another and share a school run with another. The only person to whom we can come closest to unburdening our deepest hopes and fears is our partner. This puts a great burden on close dyadic relationships; expectations are high, and for a variety of reasons – pressure of work, tiredness, post-natal depression and so forth – partners cannot always live up to them. This may explain why many divorces and partner break-ups take place. People are seeking better friends elsewhere.

As mentioned in Chapter 1, there is an argument that women now understand more about contemporary reflexive friendship than men: women meet to talk and to explore their feelings about their partners, their children and 'what it means to be a woman'. This seemingly rather narcissistic and inward-looking exploration of feelings could become obsessive and neurotic. Perhaps the Sue I have described was somewhat self-indulgent and manipulative, although she would say that more of her friends come to pour out their woes on her shoulder than vice versa. Associated with the stereotype of 'friend-rich' women is a dismissive scorn or patronizing pity for men, 'unable to share their feelings', who are limited to the cosy bonding based on beer in the public bar or claret in the Pall Mall club. The obsessive fanaticisms of engaging in or supporting sport of various kinds prevent men, so it is claimed, from, say, really getting involved with the social micro-dynamics of their seven-year-old daughter's birthday party. However, there are signs that these stereotypical views are changing as younger women become more laddish and men more openly explore 'what it means to be a man' with their friends.

Given these two persuasive alternative theories about contemporary friendship, and associated myths, fallacies and stereotypes, it is easy to see why people should be confused. Is friendship stronger now or weaker than it was . . . when? Are there truly qualitative differences between what friendship means for men and for women? And what of different classes, ethnic groups, age cohorts and so forth? Similarly, I have not referred so far to friendship between men and women. Is it true that *eros* and *amicitia* can be kept separate or must there always be an erotic element in heterosexual friendships? Do women truly find it easier to be friends with gay men or does this simply reflect anxiety about their own sexual identities?

If friendship is 'the one good thing', as Cicero claimed, is it available to all of us or are some inhibited by genetic endowment or social experience from engaging in deeply fulfilling friendships? Do we need particular kinds of close and secure relations with a mother or mother substitute to make later secure attachments to others? Are certain personality types or kinds of social experiences and contexts inimical to the development of close and mature friendships? Are those who are skilled at making such distinctive intimate bonds likely to make less satisfactory and narrowly focused partners, since the closeness they develop within their wider range of significant others distracts them from their prime bond? Or does such social capability reduce the danger of an overpressured dependence on one partner? These and many similar questions have kept generations of social psychologists and sociologists busy with their experiments and surveys.

The sociologists who describe who does what, with whom, for how long, how often, and why can provide some numerical data which may be manipulated with increasing sophistication. However, unless the dispute between the competing theories of whether we are acquiring more fragmented friends or more life-affirming soulmates is resolved, we just don't know what we are talking about. Fewer friends seen less frequently may be of far more social significance than large numbers of superficial friends.

It is indeed strange that we should still be talking past each other on the subject of friendship, despite a greater concern with the topic over the centuries than almost any other form of social relationship. We may, at present, be collectively obsessed with the social relationships between parents and children. But this was not thought to be a topic of much interest or complexity until relatively recently. Friendship, as we have seen, was of the greatest interest to classical thinkers, and the issues they raised have endured and continue to exercise the minds of contemporary philosophers. It is still refreshing to consider the continuing relevance of these philosophical issues.

The primary friendship of virtue

It is Aristotle's third type of pure friendship which requires the greatest help from philosophers. Aristotle said: 'a man stands in the same relation to his friend as to himself.'

Thus, to approve of our friend we must first approve of ourselves. Our friend, in this context becomes our 'second self'. This produces a paradox: seemingly, to be a good friend we have to have an interest in ourselves. Those who enjoy being by themselves are better equipped for showing the energy and imagination necessary in a good friend. Aristotle linked the love of friends to the love of self and the love of life. Somehow he managed to overcome the division between egoism and altruism. But philosophers quibble: how can we love a friend because he is necessary for our happiness but at the same time love that friend for his own sake? If, as seems plausible, friendship is an extension of self-love, why cannot we say that it is simply a form of narcissism and that in loving our friend we are loving ourself? But perhaps Aristotle is saying something different: perhaps he is claiming that it does not matter that friendship is linked to self-love, because that would merely demonstrate that self-love is inherently and by its very nature social. However, Aristotle does make it clear that it is only the good and virtuous who should be encouraged to be self-lovers. Vicious people must not love themselves since they will harm others by following their base feelings.

Classical writers believed that the very closest friends should share everything and also, ideally, live together. As Aristotle put it:

> clearly you cannot live with many people and distribute yourself among them . . . It is also difficult for many to share each other's enjoyments and distresses as their own, since you are quite likely to find yourself sharing one friend's pleasure and another's grief at the same time . . . it is impossible to be many people's friend for their virtue and for themselves. We have reason to be satisfied if we can find even a few such friends.

This finest and closest form of friendship, in Cicero's words:

> sends a ray of good hope into the future, and keeps our hearts from faltering or falling by the wayside. For the man who keeps his eye on a true friend, keeps it, so to speak, on a model of himself. For this reason, friends are together when they are separated, they are rich when they are poor, strong when they are weak, and – a thing even harder to explain – they live on after they have died.

These friends of virtue or friends of hope are ultimately friends of communication. Our friends who stimulate hope and invite change are concerned with deep understanding and knowing. Each grows and flourishes because of the other in a spirit of mutual awareness. As Graham Little has said in his book *Friendship: Being Ourselves with Others*, friendship is not an optional extra but the most alive of all human relationships: it is more alive than politics, markets, churches and even families and sex. It is a social sprite and can never be the 'social juggernaut' that class or race or even gender can be. Friendship has to be marginal and, indeed, somewhat subversive of the ruling beliefs of the day. Like E. M. Forster, the true friend hopes that, if forced to betray either his country or his friend, he would always choose the former. This deep communicating friend is psychologically and socially anarchistic and is qualitatively different from the friends of utility and pleasure which are more readily analysed by social scientists. Pure friendship, the friendship of character, is an alternative to society. We do not have a separate word for this deep and communicative form of friendship, but there is a Russian word, *droog*, that has connotations of Aristotle's third type of friend.

While it is helpful to go back to Aristotle and Cicero to

get a sound base for a philosophical approach to friendship, it is also helpful to consider how contemporary philosophers view the nature of intimate friendship. A good example is provided by an article published in *Ethics* (April 1998) by Dean Cocking and Jeanette Kennet. They distinguish between what they call 'the secrets view' and 'the mirror view' of friendship. According to the former view, self-disclosure cements the bonds of trust and intimacy that exist between close friends: the greater the friendship, the more we are prepared to disclose. The mirror view on the other hand is concerned with the degree to which one's own traits are reflected in the friend.

These two accounts point to different phenomena: the revealing of oneself on the one hand and the reflection of oneself on the other. In both approaches it is assumed that central to the trust and intimacy of close companionship is the disclosure of the self: either I disclose my self to the other or my self is disclosed in the other. Neither the mirror nor the secrets view is able to capture with complete success the essential features of the close or companionate style of friendship.

Close friends can open up new areas of interest, activity or intellectual concern. We may respond to our friend by exploring some new area with him; we take up an interest in orchids or contemporary poetry because that is the passion of our friend. By coming to a new interest and enjoying it, we become more like our friend. This is not because the friend is necessarily dominant or engaged in interpersonal imperialism. We are simply open to change, and the new interest may stay with us long after the friendship has ended. Another way in which friendship may change us is through the kindly truths and insights which friends may perceive about our characters, the expression of which we do not resent because we trust our friend. We may have a tendency to be pompous, to talk too much after a few drinks or whatever. Seeing ourselves through the eyes of our friend should encourage us to change or modify our behaviour. The way our friends interpret us helps us to interpret ourselves. A good friend does not stick stubbornly to a position – 'That's the sort of person I am, take it or leave it. If I offend you by speaking my mind, you'll just have to put up with it.' Some may put up with such intransigence for the sake of other benefits, but a true friendship of communication and virtue is unlikely to respond well to such rigidity. Companionable people are more open to having their interests and attitudes changed. Yet this seemingly straightforward point is counter to Aristotle's position, which is that shared activities are central and that change is more likely to threaten a friendship than to help it to grow. As Cocking and Kennet say, 'It is not that I must reveal myself to, or see myself in, the other, to any great extent, but that, in friendship, I am distinctively receptive both to the other's interests and to their way of seeing me.' My self is thus partly a product of the friendship. Of course, this is not saying much more than that the self is not a static thing. We don't acquire a friend of the soul-mate kind ready-made as it were. If our selves are changing and developing in a reciprocally rewarding and creative way, our friendship is likely to grow and flourish.

In Aristotle's view, the choosing of a friend is based on the mutual recognition of one another's virtue. This implies a fixed 'state of virtue'. So, for Aristotle, in choosing a friend we choose another self: we relate to our friend as we relate to our self. Friendship, as I have suggested, appears to be a form of self-love. This mutual acknowledgement of similarity is the Aristotelian version of the mirror view of friendship. Yet it is commonly recognized that people of strikingly different temperament and character can become close friends. Why should Aristotle insist on 'equality and likeness'?

In the case of his lesser friendship types of pleasure and utility, similarities of interest and disposition are to be expected: we choose our drinking companions from those who enjoy a drink. The mirror view might work well enough for these types but in the case of the companionship type more direction and interpretation of the one by the other would be expected. Simply having interests and 'virtue' in common cannot in themselves generate friendship: more important is that we are responsive to having our interests changed or developed. Without such responsiveness the friendship could not develop.

In the Aristotelian mirror view, I recognize much of myself in the other and I love that as I love myself. Evidently, I cannot love my friend for any traits that I cannot love in myself. If I see a reflection of some of my less-good qualities, I am likely to be less enchanted than if I recognize some of those qualities in myself of which I am most proud.

This does indeed appear to be narcissistic. Some contemporary philosophers are prepared to accept that this may be so and claim that this also characterizes Aristotle's position. Hence the importance of the argument that the mirror view is too static and passive. What we give back to our friend is not a reflection but an interpretation. Friendship is essentially a dynamic and creative process. We do not come as fully formed and self-sufficient selves into relationships. Such a view is well understood in sociology, particularly in the symbolic interaction tradition following G. H. Mead and Herbert Blumer.

Aristotle believed in the importance and pleasure in knowing ourselves: when we wish to see our face we look in the mirror. Hence the importance of the friend as a second self, reflecting us back to ourselves. Thus, he argues, 'If then it is pleasant to know oneself, and it is not possible to know this without having someone else as a friend, the self-sufficing man will require friendship in order to know himself.' Friendship is necessary to attain self-sufficiency. It is one of the arts of life. Philosophically friendship must be a dialectical process: if it were not, the dilemma arises that if one is dependent on one's friends to be self-sufficient, how could one ever claim to be self-sufficient in virtue, unless at some time one's virtue did not depend on others? I leave this for philosophers to resolve!

Before leaving this discussion of the mirror view there is the question of the friend improving our character by providing us with a view of how we should be. A friend can be like an ideal mirror, reflecting back the person she would like us to be. This would be to take a highly moralized view of friendship which is not how most people look on their closest friends.

Let us now turn to the view of friendship based on the bond of mutual trust, the secrets view, which sees self-disclosure as the crucial element in friendships of hope or character. We share confidences with our friend that we certainly would not share generally with others. Those who tell everyone everything are, as it were, disqualifying themselves from true friendship. By sharing secrets we make ourselves vulnerable to the other, which is a sign of trust and probably affection. We thereby give the friend a privileged access to influencing our lives.

But why should the sharing of secrets be so central to the notion of friendship? Some of our secrets are private or shameful, and we would be more likely go to a priest, an analyst or a complete stranger to confess them. Secrets that cause shame or embarrassment should not be imposed on one's friend. Of course friends reveal themselves to each other, but to see this as the essence of the purest type of friendship is to claim too much. Friends certainly gain great insight into each other's lives. Of greater significance is what we value and how we choose to share what we value, and this is determined in a dialectical way through the process of friendship itself.

Neither the mirror nor the secrets view provides an entirely satisfactory account of the appropriate governing conditions for friendship. Of greater importance is a more dynamic conception of friendship where each soul-mate is closely responsive to the direction and interpretation of the other. This would imply that those with more rigid personalities are simply unable to make such close friends. In his book *Autonomy and Rigid Character* David Shapiro illustrates the nature of this more rigid type:

> The fixed purposiveness of the rigid person narrows his interest in the world and restricts and prejudices his experience of it. He looks only for data – or, in the paranoid case, for clues – relevant to his purposes or concerns. The compulsive man who examines each woman with a checklist in mind of certain qualifications for marriage does not see that woman objectively; he sees a selection of traits and features whose sum is not a person but a high or low score. This is a kind of . . . awareness that is not open and attentive to the world but is restricted and prejudiced by the necessity to satisfy pre-established requirements and fixed purposes.

Such a person might have great difficulty in forming close friends or finding soul-mates. But there is no good reason, as Cocking and Kennet point out, why such a rigid person should not share secrets or be attracted by similarity in another, particularly if the other person was able to meet some of the main criteria on a checklist, as suggested above. So the secrets and mirror views of friendship cannot do much to help with the problem of the rigid person being unable to have close friends. However, the incapacity of the rigid person to be open to being directed and interpreted by others is likely to be of fundamental importance. Of course, those who are successful in drawing each other out are likely to do so more readily if they have common interests, mutual affection and a desire and interest to share each other's experiences. If one or both parties in a soul-mate dyad come to interpret their friends in too rigid a manner the friendship may fade. Family and kin relationships can survive this rigidity since they are more structured and role governed, but this would not work with companion friends, who need the flexibility and mutual drawing out to survive.

A recurrent theme from Aristotle and Cicero to contemporary writers on friendship is that our experience and exploration of what it is to be a good person is directly related to the way we behave to our closest friends. We expect our friends to be loyal, to keep confidences and to judge our behaviour according to certain standards. It is almost impossible to be friendly with someone who consistently betrays us. Betrayal and friendship cannot coexist. Many contemporary soap operas on radio and television have as their main theme the responsibilities and limits of friendship. These are frequently highly moral tales. How can we be loyal to our friend who is cheating on her partner who is also a close friend? Should you, as a friend, intervene in a situation of domestic violence when you are the only outsider who knows what is going on? The agony columns of newspapers and magazines provide a stream of examples. It is among our closest friends that we work out together what the 'right' thing to do might be. Part of the function of friendship is to provide the anvil on which we may individually beat out our own personal moralities. In this sense, friendship is a metaphor for morality. How to be a good and dutiful daughter, wife or mother is less likely to be discussed with a mother, husband or daughter than with a friend.

Yet some argue that it is now more difficult to make and nurture friends: Henrik Ibsen wrote: 'Friends are a costly luxury. When a man invests his capital of energy in a profession or a mission, he will lack the means to afford friends.' We know that friends may be important for us morally, emotionally and practically. However, in a society where loneliness can lead to clinical depression and the physical health of the elderly can be worse for the friendless, ways of encouraging friends and friendship is of great social importance.

Friendship in decline or friendship at the core?

Are we creating a world, at least for the overwork committed senior salariat, where we do not have the time and energy to practice one of the fundamental arts of life? Friendship requires time for it to flourish and develop. It is essentially about talk and communication. Some argue that the complexities arising from serial monogamy, tiring journeys to work, more demanding and stressful work situations, more demanding and stressful parenting, caring, and so much else besides mean that the close sharing friendship that I have been discussing in this chapter is itself too demanding. Those with equal burdens in employment are kept apart by similar time constraints. Those with unequal time burdens are unlikely to form close friendships: the one with the greater time will be perceived by the other as too demanding. If one is already suffering from emotional overload then a call late at night from a friend with relationship problems may be the last straw. Some people cannot be good friends. 'God protect me from my friends', they complain. 'I need space and a bit of peace for myself.' So, with a fairly straight face, can one say that globalization, consumerism and family-caring responsibilities are killing friendship? Or, perhaps more subtly, does our great freedom to choose our friends lead to a lack of constraint over the accumulation of greedy and demanding friends?

In a survey about friendship networks carried out in North London in the mid-1980s, Peter Willmott showed, without being too precise about the meaning of the term, that the category 'friend' was more important than those of 'relative' or 'neighbour' for helping with shopping, house maintenance, 'keeping an eye on the house' and personal advice. There are also indications that while regular visits to family and kin are declining, those regular visits to friends, though they are also declining, are declining less rapidly. If friends are becoming more important than family and kin in certain respects, it is less easy to be sure why this may be so. On the one hand, the identity that friends are able to bestow on us may be more important than the ascribed identities of mother, daughter, sibling, or whatever. While, as we have seen in the case of Sue, an ascribed relation can develop if an achieved friend-like relative is imposed upon it, this is unusual. We value those friends and friend-like relations who affirm the view of ourselves that we most wish to be. A number of sociological studies, including that by Peter Willmott, mentioned above, consistently emphasized the importance of friends as sources of emotional support and advice.

On the balance between *philia* and *eros*

While many people recognize the social and economic pressures that take time away from the cultivation of friendship, they would argue that their best, and perhaps only, friend is their partner. Perhaps the phrase 'just friends' as a euphemism for *not* sleeping together is changing in meaning. This is an interesting area where the social mores appear to be in flux. On the one hand there is the transition from beginning as friends and turning into lovers, and on the other hand there is the transition from being lovers and ending as friends. Can the two really go together? In a survey carried out by the magazine *Psychology Today* in 1979, just under one-third of both men and women said that they had had sexual intercourse with a friend in the past month. Respondents were heavily skewed towards those under thirty-five and not too much should be made of such findings, given that we do not know how the word 'friend' should be unpacked. However, I have little doubt that there is a contemporary view that sexual love and pure friendship can fruitfully co-exist. Perhaps it is the existence of such a belief that encourages some to divorce, seeking the ever-elusive magic combination elsewhere.

In the 1989 film *When Harry Met Sally*, the two principal protagonists are driving together in the opening scene from Chicago to New York and Harry remarks 'Men and women can't be friends – because the sex part gets in the way.' Many contemporary philosophers would agree, claiming that love is essentially possessive which is inimical to the pure form of friendship of virtue. Harry elaborates his point when he meets Sally five years later and modifies his original rule by adding, 'unless both are involved with other people'. However, he goes on: 'But that doesn't work. The person you are involved with can't understand why you need to be friends with the other person. She figures you must be secretly interested in the other person – which you probably are. Which brings us back to the first rule.' In philosophical terms the problems of combining *eros* and *philia* are not easily resolvable. In common experience there are many who would agree with Harry, but equally there are many who would strongly disagree, pointing to many historical and literary hetero-sexual friendships as illustrations of the highest form of Aristotelian friendship.

Because friends and friendship appear to offer more freedom and choice they may seem to provide more space and scope for individual identity and autonomy. The flight from dependency in personal relations is surely healthy. However, the key issue remains: if friends should not be lovers, can, or should, spouses or partners be friends? Whatever the philosophers say, the answer surely must be yes. However, for this to happen men and women have to recognize their other selves: men have to become more confident with their *anima* and women with their *animus*. This will not be easy. Society does so much to emphasize gender differences. When men and women find in their partner another self, another individuality but one whose otherness is not so overwhelming as to threaten or engulf or invade their selfhood, they are truly fortunate. In his essay *Talking* J. B. Priestley handles the balance between *eros* and *philia* very effectively: initially, for the friendship between the two individuals to develop, sex must be relegated to the background. Each has to recognize the individuality of the other and respond to the other in the ways I have discussed above. But then Priestley goes on to point out that, having recognized how alike they are as men and women, they 'will then go forward . . . [and] discover how unlike the sexes are. . . . This double play of personality, and then of sex, is what gives intelligent talk between men and women its curious piquancy.' In this sense friendship between the sexes may take us not out of ourselves but beyond ourselves and may make us more whole, balanced and sane than we could otherwise be.

But friendship in marriage or long-term relationships cannot be presumed. Men fear engulfment; a woman fears an invasiveness that threatens the boundary she has struggled to maintain between herself and others. Each is tempted to shy away from otherness and settle for friends more like the self: women to women friends, men to their men friends. Perhaps *eros* is necessary to overcome such fears, hesitation and timidity. *Eros* may be the trigger that helps some men and women to discover true friendship. To quote J. B. Priestley again:

> Talk demands that people should begin, as it were, at least some distance from one another, that there should be some doors still to unlock. Marriage is partly the unlocking of those doors, and it sets out on its happiest and prosperous voyages when it is launched on floods of talk.

Communicating friendship is one of the great arts of living, even though by drawing us together it may be a form of social regression, as Philip Slater has argued. There is much in the modern world that prevents us from having the time and emotional security to be a true friend. Our hopes and aspirations are raised and we may be deluded into believing that there are short cuts. But the 'one good thing' of communicating friendship is trivialized and demeaned by the superficial glad-handedness of much corporate culture. The ever-spiralling, first-name-calling networkers are the enemies of true friendship. They take up our time and lure us to the popular crowd at the symbolic bars of life. However, true friendship as an essential ingredient of the art of life needs to be respected and nourished.

The dialectics of friendship

How friendship may be effectively nourished is discussed by William Rawlins in *Friendship Matters*. He is a specialist in interpersonal and relational communication and his work focuses precisely on Aristotle's communicative form of pure friendship. He puts his main emphasis on the interactive and dialectical aspects of friendship. He suggests that this dialectical tension arises out of a specific category of relationship within contemporary middle-class American culture and that such tensions are inherent in the actual communicative practices occurring between friends. As he puts it: 'I attempt to portray the various degrees of involvement, enjoyment, choice, risk, ambivalence, ambiguity, practicality and emotion of friendship in negotiating self-conceptions and human relationships within given yet revisable social matrices.' (As Mark Twain may have said, 'Good music is a hell of a lot better than it sounds.')

Nevertheless, it is worth discussing Rawlins's four dialectical processes in some detail:

1) *The dialectic of the freedom to be independent and the freedom to be dependent*
On the one hand, one expects to be free to pursue one's life and personal interests, without necessarily having any interference or help from one's friend. However, one also wants to have the freedom to call or to rely on one's friend in times of need. Both forms of freedom involve choices, and the result of these choices impinges on the other's choice. Each individual friendship is likely to emphasize

different aspects of the dialectic. These contradictory free-
doms have to be endlessly negotiated. Independence from
a friend may be more valued when the option of dependence is also maintained. Similarly, the privilege of
depending on someone is more likely to be appreciated
when one feels that one's autonomy is also being
respected. Sharing these two forms of freedom helps to
bind friends together. Clearly, complete independence
would imply no relationship at all, whereas total dependence would constrain both parties by undermining their
individual integrity and autonomy.

2) *The dialectic of affection and instrumentality*
The tensions between generosity or altruism and reciprocity or between spontaneity and obligation have to be
resolved. The assumption is that true friendship is more
appropriately based on affection than on instrumentality,
which is related to 'false' forms of friendship. Yet, as
Rawlins points out, that is oversimple, since 'selfishness
draws individuals towards friends and generosity attracts
friends to persons.' Evidently fears of inadvertent exploi-
tation and/or indebtedness could be disruptive. If one
friend felt that the other's concern or aid was habitually
obligatory or offered out of duty, it would evidently sour
or undermine the friendship. Once the idea of equivalence
enters a friendship it will surely start to die. It is quite
acceptable for a friend to be totally instrumental at times
in asking another for favours. Indeed, some very close
friends recognize others' rather blatant manipulation of
good will and generosity, but with deep and underlying
affection a relationship will be recognized in the round.
The total, unconditional acceptance of the other – warts
and all – is often the way people refer to their ideal of a
best friend. To practise strict reciprocity would be a
burden, as would unstinted and unquestioning altruism.

This raises problems for friends who may be suddenly physically incapacitated and then have to accept more affection than the previous pattern of the friendship would support. The tensions and difficulties of this dialectic can be more readily accommodated over a friendship that stretches well over the life-course. One way to show this is in the form of figure 1.

Figure 1

		Commitment/Obligation	
		High	Low
Attachment/Affection	High	1	2
	Low	3	4

In the case of box 3 the obligation is higher but the affection is low, and this might spell the end of the friendship. However, if at a previous stage in the life-course the two friends were in box 1, box 3 would be supportable. Of course each party to the friendship will be allocated to the appropriate box separately. One friend in box 1 could get on reasonably well with a friend in Box 2 because of the strength of the emotional attachment. Readers can work out appropriate combinations for themselves and recognize that, over a long period of friendship, individuals could move between all the boxes, sometimes synchronized with the other, sometimes not.

The interweaving of these contradictory dimensions of affection and obligation may help to distinguish different types of friend. Different trajectories through the life-course will help to give the friendship something of its distinctive style and flavour. Charlotte Brontë's comment at the head of this chapter suggests well the delicate balance inherent in this dialectic.

3) *The dialectic of judgement and affection*

People are at ease with their friends when they believe that they are liked and accepted by someone familiar with both their strengths and their weaknesses. They know that when they are charming and cheery they make good company, but most people also have irritating habits and compulsions. Even if a friend is judgemental sometimes, at least he implies that the other is being treated seriously. Sometimes the true friend will be prepared to turn a blind eye to the other's failings, and some would say that this is a basic requirement of intimacy. As Rawlins says, acceptance functions in a dialectic relationship with the friends' judgements. 'People value a friend's acceptance, especially when they know the other takes their ideas, thoughts and actions seriously.' Criticism and judgement is acceptable from someone who primarily accepts and cares for the other.

4) *The dialectic of expressiveness and protectiveness*

There is a clear tension between the impulse to be open and expressive but also to protect sensitive parts of the self. Friends have to learn to avoid hurting each other, to preserve confidences and to exercise restraint in probing sensitive areas. Clearly, trust is of the essence here. As Rawlins puts it, 'self limits self's own vulnerability and strives to protect other's sensitivities whilst still expressing thoughts and feelings.' Friends want to trust in the honesty of each other's comments but they also trust them not to be hurtful by being too blunt. We have to put limits on our own vulnerability by what we can expect of ourselves, and we must also protect our friends' sensitivities. Honesty must be matched with tact and discretion.

I have dwelt at some length and put my own interpretation on these dialectics because they serve a very useful purpose in showing how the notion of communicating friendship can be unpacked. These are the stock-in-trade of those teaching communicative skills, but it is important to remember that those who are able to be 'good friends' have certain skills and qualities that do make them different. We develop our own sense of who we are by the way we develop our friendships. Some people are able to do this intuitively, but it is as well to remember that, with a degree of self-consciousness, it is possible to be a better friend. This is a lesson that boys and men seem, in general, to have to learn more than women, as the novel *White City Blue*, discussed above, illustrated so well.

Many sociologists would argue that identity is becoming increasingly fluid and variable. More than ever before *Le style est l'homme même*. The previous main determinants of identity – family and work – are changing in ways that are becoming increasingly familiar. Women are perhaps more practised at developing non-occupationally based identities and men may be finding it more difficult. With more flexible employment practices, the collapse of the psychological contract and what may be termed 'the privatization of the CV', as personnel management has been replaced by human resource management, and with a widespread move to self-employment, men's range of work experiences may be very diverse. Their position in society may be more quickly and neatly established by the clothes they wear, the car they drive, the area where they live and how they furnish and decorate their homes. However, to reveal the right signs, symbols, labels, makes, marks and combinations means nothing unless they are recognized. The status, the identity, the sense of self is not bestowed by the objects but by the recognition of the objects by others.

Kaeren Harrison, in her study of middle-class women, already referred to in Chapter 1, concluded:

with friends they believed they could be 'authentic', find and create new identities and present a number of alternative aspects of self.

She further quotes one of the contributors to the Mass Observation Archive at Sussex University, who sums up rather well the relationships between partner, friends and the self:

> With my husband, I feel I have to tread carefully, as he construes some things as criticisms of himself. He doesn't think others are worth talking about and says so, so I tend to censor what I say – think first, plan a diplomatic way of putting things, i.e. not speaking too impulsively. The point is, with friends, all that doesn't matter. With friends, it is much easier to relax and let the 'true self' show.

4

Friendship in Context

> In Mali, best friends throw excrement at each other
> and comment loudly on the genitals of their respec-
> tive parents – this to us unnatural and obscene
> behaviour is a proof of the love of friends.
>
> Robert Brain, *Friends and Lovers*

Friendship changes in its meaning and function through the life-course. This may seem a palpably obvious and unexceptional statement, but, as sociologists and social psychologists have shown, the social significance of the word 'friend' is so different as we go through the life-course that scholarly interests have had to become highly specialized in order to understand it. For reasons of space, anthropological studies of friendship in non-Western cultures are not considered in this chapter.

There are distinct literatures concerned with problems at different stages of life: social psychologists have studied mainly the problems of childhood and adolescence. During their early socialization at school children learn the rules, attitudes and obligations of what it is to be a good friend. This early learning period, it is said, helps to form notions of fairness and, ultimately, what it means to be a good citizen. During adolescence forming close and intimate friends is a very important part of discovering and developing one's self and in making the psychological break from one's parents. Women use other female friends to help them come to terms with motherhood and being a partner. Friendship in old age has considerable significance for health and well-being and social policy issues have prompted substantial research in this area. Scholars have specialized in different age stages and there are also a number of textbooks and specialized reviews of the literature on the topic of friendship through the life-course. What follows is, perforce, highly selective.

Sociologists have traditionally been more concerned with the structural and contextual factors affecting friendship. Different styles and patterns of friendship have been documented for different levels of the social structure and these, in turn, are affected by race, gender and ethnicity. A previously rather static view of friendship describing so-called 'working-class' patterns of friendship and contrasting these with so-called 'middle-class' patterns of friendship, has been replaced by a more dynamic and context-focused view. As Graham Allan, the doyen of English studies of friendship, remarked, 'Friendships . . . are the product of their time and place.' The old, rather simplified stereotypes have collapsed in the face of the demographic, material and social changes that grew in force through the twentieth century. Much of the ethnographic material on friendship was based on studies of particular localities or occupational communities. With deindustrialization, social and geographical mobility and all the other ingredients of social turbulence, these previous ethnographic studies are now more of historical interest and do little to help us understand the dynamics of the current situation. We shall return to this theme later.

This chapter is inevitably something of a taster to a whole range of problems and issues surrounding the notion of friendship. It cannot be comprehensive, and those wishing to be more systematic are encouraged to follow up the further reading suggested at the end.

Children's friendships

The work of social and developmental psychologists, which has focused on children's friendships over the past thirty years or so, owes much to the pioneering work of Jean Piaget, who published *The Moral Judgement of the Child* in 1932. Piaget claimed that children's orientation towards moral issues mirrors the structure of their most important social relationships. His assumption was that these would initially be with adults, who would provide the rules for the child's behaviour. However, as children grow older and spend more time with their peers, they discover a different model for social relationships. When among other children it is clear that no child can claim authority to make the rules. Hence, young children in the company of their peers begin to exchange ideas and gradually develop friendships based on discussion, reciprocity and mutual respect. According to Piaget, they come to understand that equality is the most critical element of fairness.

Children first use the term 'friend' from the age of about three or four. At this stage, according to development psychologists, a friend is mainly a playmate who is conveniently nearby. The child is not yet able to distinguish their own perspective from that of others or to recognize that the other may perceive the same events and circumstances in a different way. The intrusion of another child in the play or feelings of jealousy connected with the commandeering of specific toys will simply lead to squabbles over these toys or space or whatever, rather than the conflicts involving personal feelings of loyalty, trust or affection.

Continuing this model devised by developmental psychologists, it is claimed that between the ages of about four and seven, children gradually perceive that their own perspectives and that of others may differ and that each person has an individual, unique personal psychic identity. However, friends are seen as important suppliers of assistance. They can perform specific activities that fit in with what is demanded. 'Knowing' a friend well would imply an accurate knowledge of what the other liked or disliked and what could be, as it were, supplied to them.

A third stage develops between the ages of six and twelve when children begin to be able to put themselves in the other's shoes. By being able to take a second person's perspective, it is possible to move on to reciprocities of thought and feelings, rather than simply those of actions alone. Some adjustment is possible, recognizing that the other may have specific likes and dislikes. Nevertheless, the ties binding the two together have no great strength and arguments are likely to lead to amicable break-ups of the 'friendship'. This has been described as the stage of fair-weather co-operation. As the child gets older – between the ages of nine and fifteen – a qualitatively new stage is reached. Here the child is able to move out of an interpersonal interaction and both recognize and co-ordinate the perspectives of each of them. By being thus able to take a third party perspective, a new awareness emerges, enabling a continuity of relationships and affective bonding among close friends. Friends at this stage are able to give each other mutual support, to share with each other their personal problems and to recognize a degree of possessiveness. The understanding that close friendly relations require effort, both to develop and to maintain, implies a move beyond fair-weather co-operation to the beginnings of real commitment.

The final stage of autonomous and independent friendship can begin as early as the age of twelve and continues into adulthood. Those who reach this stage recognize that their friends are also closely linked with others in their own individual personal communities. There is a realization that the individual friendship is part of a larger societal network of relationships. Dependence and independence are perceived as having a dialectical relationship with each other. Friends rely on each other both for support and for a sense of personal identity, but also accept that each needs the space to develop relationships with others. There follows a growth in maturity through such experiences.

While there may not be complete agreement about the precise number and content of these developmental levels and stages of friendship, it is generally accepted by psychologists that what it means to be a friend evolves and increases in intensity through childhood. Given this, developmental psychologists claim that competency in developing mature relationships in childhood will bear some relationship with adult adjustments and capacities to make and maintain mature relationships. Do well-adjusted children make well-adjusted adults? Could it, perhaps, be demonstrated that the feelings of social competence and the bolstering of feelings of self-esteem as a child could lead to more secure and lasting couple bonding or more effective competence at the workplace later on in life?

These are heady possibilities: crudely, make better friends as a child and you will be a happier and more sociable adult, with less chance of stressful divorce or similar emotional break-ups. Certainly psychologists such as Harry Stack Sullivan have claimed that failing to form a close friendship in pre-adolescence may lead to feelings of loneliness later on in life. Perhaps greater effectiveness as an adult in friendly and romantic relationships can be predicted from the knowledge of the subject's pre-adolescent friendships, which may serve as building blocks for future relationships. Thus, it may be that children who appear to lack the necessary skills to form mature friendships will continue to have difficulties in forming high-quality adult friendships later in life. This would imply that the enduring communicative friendship which philosophers endlessly seek to define may not be available to all adults who are, as it were, 'close-friend challenged'. It is important not to accept the seemingly plausible assumptions of the psychologists too readily.

Plainly, rigorous empirical testing of these suggestions is not easy. It would involve a long-term longitudinal study with a very complex research design. Evidence appears to suggest that general rejection by peers at school *does* lead to long-term consequences, both in terms of educational success and later deviant behaviour. However, the evidence for the long-term implications of success in developing friendship leading to mental-health adjustment is not so clear. There is little doubt that children with friends at each developmental stage are likely to have greater self-esteem and that more mature friendships provide a context for self-disclosure, mutual understanding and emotional support. It is also generally recognized that adult friends may provide an important buffer against stress and that this may serve as a protection against later depressive feelings prompted by stressful life situations.

However, it has to be acknowledged that it is too early to say whether such suppositions can be firmly substantiated. Lacking friends and being rejected by peers in childhood may be only symptoms of other, more complex, behavioural and adjustment difficulties. Some other disturbance could be the cause of difficulties both with children and with adults. Hence, it must be accepted that, at present, robust causal links between pre-adolescent peer and friendship relations and other adult behaviour cannot be made. Research on this topic will surely continue, but in the meantime it would be dangerous to stigmatize solitary children as 'faulty interactants' – to take a rather unpleasant phrase from Erving Goffman.

Despite such general caution, there have been some interesting attempts to focus on specific aspects of early friendships and to relate these to specific outcomes. One such example explored the way friendship affected social interaction and early literacy learning. Friends were shown to generate more literate language than non-friends – the mutuality and trust that characterizes friendships appear to encourage children to engage in intellectual disagreement and resolutions. Thus, it seems likely that the quality of individual friendships is more supportive in developing early literacy than simply the possession of a number of friends: 'the best friend' dyad is probably of greater salience for supporting effective cognitive processing.

A cavalier attitude to social context in much psychological research makes generalization very problematic. What it means to be a friend is a matter for research, not a matter of course. In nearly all the psychological studies, despite their being generally carried out with all the 'scientific' trappings of rigorous sampling and statistical analysis, in the words of Thomas Berndt, a critic from within:

> Investigators treated friendship in very superficial terms. Despite liberal use of the word 'friends' in both title and text, their articles focused on determinants of status among one's peers. 'Friendship' was merely a vehicle for measuring popularity.

Researchers often focused on 'connectedness' – that is, the degree to which an individual was accepted by peers and tied into a social network. Given the common-sense view that disturbed adults have a long-standing history of peer relations indicating low acceptance, educationists and psychologists may try to boost a child's 'sociometric ratings'. But, to quote the previous critic again, 'Friendship has been presented in superficial terms, as if the important thing is to be connected to others, regardless of the content of such connections.'

Without delving too deeply into these methodological niceties, which can lead to acrimonious interdisciplinary sniping, it is worth referring to one pioneering classic study carried out in the 1950s by the American psychologist Merrill Roff. Roff was working with American servicemen and he was able to locate those who in middle childhood had been referred to guidance clinics in Minnesota and who were later diagnosed by military psychiatrists as neurotic or psychotic or given a dishonourable discharge for antisocial conduct. The child clinic records of these servicemen were then compared with those of former clinic patients who had exemplary later military records. Disordered servicemen were found to be anywhere between two and four times as likely as nondisordered servicemen to have had a history of poor peer relations. There seems little doubt from this and other studies that disordered individuals have a history of peer disturbance.

Some years later, Roff and other colleagues used a sample of 38,000 children in Texas and Minnesota and followed sub-samples over a four-year period from the third to the sixth stage of school. This overcame some of the problems of the earlier study, since clearly a sample selected through child-guidance clinics cannot be representative of the general population. Only male respondents were selected, and information on peer adjustment was based on teachers' observations – evidently largely qualitative and subjective. The later, larger project was exceptionally carefully and rigorously planned and executed.

The conclusions of this important study carry a crucial message to educationists, child psychologists and policy makers in general. The authors moved a long way from the traditional and somewhat blinkered psychological perspective, which attempts to isolate the study of social acceptance from its context:

> Peer rejection is more often the lot of the less fortunate, the less able, the less effective and the socially less advantaged ... Peer acceptance was found to be positively associated with higher socio-economic status, higher intelligence, higher educational level of parents, loving and casual parental attitudes, better health and a number of other positive background factors.

Despite Roff's warnings, which to a degree undermine his own findings, psychologists persist in carrying out studies of peer acceptance with scant regard for 'background factors' and, when reporting the results, conflate friendship with peer acceptance.

The search for unequivocal links between childhood friendship and adult behaviour continues unabated among psychologists. Research reported in the journal *Child Development* in 1998 attempted to test precisely the thesis of the distinguished American psychologist Harry Stack Sullivan that pre-adolescent friendships have long-term implications for an individual's feelings of competence and self-worth. The sense of self-worth, which comes from the social reciprocities of friendship, is held to be important in dealing with the problems associated with puberty and significant school transitions. The original sample had a mean age of 10.3 years, representing over 90 per cent of the fifth grade students in five elementary schools in a suburban midwestern community. A follow-up study of sixty young adults was carried out, matching those who had a stable mutual best friend in the fifth grade with a chumless group of those who did not receive a reciprocal nomination by any of their three best friend choices at the fifth grade assessments. The mean age of the young adults was 23.2 years.

The authors went to considerable lengths to make sure that the selection of these two groups was done rigorously to ensure the later validity of their results. Not surprisingly, perhaps, those pre-adolescents with friends had more prominent reputations than the chumless peers. The 23 year olds who had had a stable mutual friend when they were ten years old looked back with much more positive feelings on that period than those who were chumless at the time. However, the crucial question, of course, is whether their experiences twelve years previously had any direct consequences for their present emotional situation and their success in the intervening period. There does seem to have been a clear association between pre-adolescent friendship and positive relations with family members. Furthermore, Sullivan's thesis seems to be generally supported, in that feelings of positive self-esteem as a young adult appeared to be well predicted by pre-adolescent friendship status. Likewise, a presence of depressive symptomology in adulthood is uniquely associated with a failure to form a close friendship in pre-adolescence.

However, the further assumption that young adults would also be more confident in their friendly and romantic relationships if they had a positive pre-adolescent friendship experience was, surprisingly, not supported by the data. Similarly, peer rejection did not seem to make a difference either. The development of a robust causal model is not yet possible, and the authors had to face the possibility that lacking friends and being rejected by the peer group in pre-adolescence might only be markers for behavioural and adjustment difficulties and therefore have no implications for maladjustment in adults.

Given the care and determination of the authors to select a valid sample and to carry out a follow-up study after twelve years, it is disappointing that the results remain less conclusive than might be expected, particularly in the context of the amount of research devoted to this area of developmental psychology over the past fifty years. A number of other studies, however, have shown a relationship between pre-adolescent peer rejection and later psychopathological symptoms, and so research studies will continue – doubtless at ever-increasing costs.

To establish causal links in this area obviously poses enormous practical problems of research design – whether this is to be prospective or retrospective. Surprisingly, the psychologists who were authors of the longitudinal study under discussion did not include a measure of friendship quality when they studied the pre-adolescents. There is frequently an assumption in psychological research that 'having friends' in fact implies 'having supportive friendships of high quality' (however that might be interpreted for a ten- or eleven-year-old). A failure to make this distinction probably invalidates much research of the meaning and significance of friends and friendship among children and their effects on later life experiences.

Thomas Berndt, in a recent review, discusses the great difficulties in exploring the effect of friendship quality. He criticizes the classic statements of Piaget and Sullivan for the limitations of their differing views of 'quality'. Piaget emphasized the importance of equality in friendship relationships as being central to moral development. Sullivan considered friendships to be high in quality when they were high in intimacy and collaboration but low in competition.

So what precise features of friendship are intrinsic to friendship quality among children and how should they be measured? Furthermore, how should certain specific features be correlated with which other specific features of social development? It is clear that, even in the late 1990s, psychologists were having enormous difficulty in resolving these issues. Berndt points out that researchers often limit themselves to the positive features of friendship, which follows much classical writing on friendship. Yet when children are asked about problems in their friendships they frequently report conflicts, unpleasant competition and rivalries. To describe friendships accurately, both the positive and negative aspects have to be precisely described and balanced with each other. Secondly, counter to Piaget's assumption, equality is not a given in children's friendships. Individuals frequently compete with each other and one friend may dominate or boss the other one around. Thirdly, the positive and negative aspects of friendship define separate dimensions of friendship, which have been found to be only weakly correlated. Psychologists, obliged to respect the conventional cannon of scientific (i.e. precisely measured) research, must then determine some kind of composite score.

In addition, every friendship involves two people who may differ and disagree about the quality of their respective relationship with each other. Also, it cannot be assumed that adolescents can have only one 'best friend'. Clearly, some have a number of 'best friends'. How are the singles and multiples to be accommodated in the same research design?

The second half of the problem relates to which aspects

of social development should be taken as measures to correlate with friendship quality? And can it necessarily be assumed that the direction of causality is from friendship quality to psychological adjustment when the reverse may be easily plausible? If, as Berndt asserts, researchers have consistently failed to obtain support for plausible hypotheses relating to friendship quality, is this simply a matter of poor research design? Would not better, carefully constructed longitudinal studies provide definitive answers? The impact of quality friendship on an adolescent's life may have different short-term and long-term consequences. In the short-term a friend may simply serve to avoid boredom on a particular day, but in the long-term may do much to increase interpersonal competence. 'During interactions with a good friend', Berndt suggests, 'a child may learn the social skills needed for initiating interactions with peers, carrying on an intimate conversation, and resolving conflicts with others.' However, the distinction between the immediate impact and the formative impact is not absolute. Finally, Berndt suggests that observation of actual friendly behaviour is vital. It is truly astonishing that most psychologists should be so slow in recognizing the stock-in-trade of social anthropology and sociology. Berndt claims that the connections between abstract features of friendship and actual behaviour 'are virtually unknown'. This is a surprising conclusion for him to come to after a review of voluminous literature on friendship and social development stretching over thirty years.

The rich tapestry of
ethnographical reporting

If the problem with the psychologists was the limitations of their narrow focus, sociologists and social anthropologists in their descriptive studies open up a colourful kaleidoscope of forms and styles of friendship, and, of course, novelists and film-makers also provide complex and multi-stranded insights. Here the problem is the danger of being overwhelmed by rich and varied ethnography. Many small-scale studies of teenagers, twenty-somethings and thirty-somethings often do no more than reflect the various TV soaps that are focused on the dramas of everyday life. The problem of asserting a gay or lesbian identity that is counter to the expectation of parents and family often leads to a heavy reliance on friends – 'the family' of the gay community. Young women seeking to assert their own independence in the early years of feminism relied hugely on particular friends for support and in these cases friends came to complement and sometimes supplant family ties.

Young teenage girls have been described as more home-based than boys, spending time with two or three friends, listening to records and talking about boys and pop stars. Angela McRobbie coined the phrase 'bedroom culture' in the 1970s to describe this phase and drew a distinction between this more private world and that of the gangs of mates with whom boys hang out. However, the rapidly shifting teenage cultural scene makes many ethnographic accounts outdated almost as soon as they are published. In a recent postgraduate thesis, teenagers in Nottingham were interviewed by a student at Manchester University. One of these, Danielle, who had just started socializing, explained that the experience of frequently 'getting drunk with your friends makes you closer.' Another teenager, William, remarked, 'The whole drinking and club scene has made our friendships stronger; we go out and have a laugh. There's more chance to talk. Before we'd just played football.'

A variety of fragmentary evidence from journalists, and also modest sociological studies such as those mentioned above, suggest that the rather marked gender differences and patterns of teenage friendship reported in earlier studies may be breaking down. The centrality of talk in friendship is coming to be equally important for both boys and girls. However, there are still substantial regional and class differences. Young people in higher education are likely to have close friends covering a broad spread of class backgrounds and sexual orientations. Young male manual workers, by contrast, are still likely to be limited to their mates and would rarely expect to have a young woman as a friend – unless, possibly, a sister, fills this role.

Sociologists have extended the range of accounts of forms of friendship in different contexts but they are often as cavalier about the actual quality of the relationships they describe as are the developmental psychologists. Elision between 'friends' and 'peer group' is common. Funding bodies are interested in supporting research to find out what encourages young people to take up smoking, regular and harmful drinking and drugs. It is not particularly surprising to discover that 'friends' are important. However, there are, of course, friends and friends – those who support socially approved forms of behaviour being more desirable in the eyes of moral guardians than those who are more adventurous in breaking societal norms.

Adolescence and early adulthood is a period when young people learn about being a friend and experiment with different styles of friendship. This process can go on until the early twenties, as different identities are practised in front of different audiences. This is a crucial period for developing social competence, and it has been claimed that should things go wrong at this crucially formative period there may be consequences that will reverberate throughout a person's life. The classic statement of this idea by Erik Erikson in 1968 is worth recalling:

> Where a youth does not accomplish such intimate relation-ships with others – and, I would add, with his own inner resources – in late adolescence or early adulthood, he may settle for highly stereotyped interpersonal relations and come to retain a deep *sense of isolation*. If the times favour an impersonal kind of interpersonal pattern a man [sic] can go far, very far in life and yet harbour a severe character problem, doubly painful because he will never feel really himself, although everyone says he is 'somebody'.

Having a close, character-making friend, based on open communication, is likely to be far more significant and important for an individual's future development than simply being surrounded by peers – the crowd, the gang, the mates, or whatever. The crucial importance of friend-ship quality, to which we so frequently return, is of course very difficult to measure, and researchers easily slip into conscious or unconscious subjective value judgements.

Sociologists have been ready to make very wide-ranging generalizations about men's friendship patterns and women's friendship patterns. Men were held to be emo-tionally reticent – fearful, perhaps, of homoerotic over-tones, while women were held to be more articulate and emotionally accomplished. Hence, class and gender stere-otypes were constructed on the basis of a number of small case studies. In the traditional working class, it was claimed, men did not disclose their innermost feelings but talked overwhelmingly about work and sport or pigeons and fishing. If they used the word 'friend' it was in terms of someone they did things with. The other side of the cliché was the world of more articulate women, who gossiped, explored feelings and analysed the micro-dynamics of family life with subtlety and sophistication.

In the middle class, by contrast, the gender differences were said to be less sharp. Heterosexual friendships were possible but limited to more artistic and bohemian circles. Of course, it was appreciated that within the middle class there was considerable variation. At the lower end, enter-taining was limited, constrained on the one hand by status anxiety and the need to preserve social distance from the working class. Higher status 'friends' would be sought as symbols and referents of social position. However, at a time when lower-middle-class women were primarily housewives, financial constraints on the household made it difficult for them to keep up with higher-status and more affluent 'friends'. Such social markers could rarely become close and communicative friends. Women were more likely to confide in their siblings who, in this way, became more friend-like. Their financial strength of the more established, professional middle class, by contrast, ensured good protection from interlopers from below, who had neither the material nor the social resources to match those above them and so were unable to maintain that level of entertaining. Typically, at dinner parties women would exercise carefully acquired skills in 'drawing out' their male partners or perhaps, somewhat daringly, engaging in some mild flirtation. However, real friend-type conversation had to wait until they had left the men to their port and retired to the drawing room.

In many ways, the upper-middle class style was closer to the working-class pattern of gender segregated worlds than to the more cosy lower middle class. The Pall Mall clubs and the working men's clubs had more in common

than their respective members imagined. In both the
established upper middle class and the traditional working
class, kinship links took up most available social time.
Among the working class, aunties, uncles, cousins, nans
and plenty of small children kept everyone busy and
involved with each other and there was little time, space
or resources for other friends. Similarly, in the upper
middle class, more likely to be scattered around the
country, there was much visiting and staying at each
other's houses. Marriages, funerals, baptisms and significant birthdays and other anniversaries were all occasions
for tribal gatherings. When one well-established family
intermarried with another and got on well, the social
calendar could get very crowded. Country cottages would
be filled with relatives and selected friends for the young
at holiday time but close, communicating adult friends
outside the family were relatively rare. Friend-like
relationships developed more readily with agnatic or
affinal kin.

Between these two stereotypical extremes there was a
large middle mass where friendship was, as I have suggested, frequently a source of anxiety. Friends might make
social demands that could not be reciprocated or might
be unsuitable in other ways. The world of privatized mid-
century middle England could not afford to be particularly
friendly. Countless novels explore the nuances of this
situation.

For different reasons, those in the lowest class category
had, so it was argued, neither the material resources nor
the social skills to sustain close friendships. Life in the
slums or among the itinerant rural poor, it was suggested,
was too impoverished in every way.

These then, were just some of the clichés of class and
gender that were elaborated and embellished by novelists

and certain sociologists from the 1920s to the 1970s. Yet at the same time there were completely contrary accounts which made the clichés seem misleadingly superficial. Some autobiographies of working-class men who had been highly socially mobile – such as that by Ralph Glasser, who grew up in the Gorbals, a notorious Glasgow slum – showed that some working-class young men had intense communicative friendships, sharing their innermost thoughts and exploring with great sensitivity their innermost feelings. Furthermore, these autobiographies referred to the social worlds of their siblings and peers who, while not necessarily socially mobile, still sometimes had true friendships of virtue. Again, oral history has revealed intense friendships between men during the century's two main wars. Men, forced together in the horrific circumstances of active service, expressed feelings of love towards each other with a tenderness and sympathy that was in no way inferior to the greatest love and friendship between women. Working-class men, perhaps, liberated in their common interdependence from the anxieties of homoeroticism, allowed the expression of deep and warm feelings to each other. There were also close and warm links across the various class divisions. Likewise, the liberation of women from domesticity encouraged the emergence of more mate-like behaviour among women workers who might go out drinking or on trips to the seaside in a particularly boisterous way.

Finally, a more sympathetic exploration of the privatized lower middle class revealed great areas of friendship among sub-groups such as the Methodists, who made friendship, particularly between couples, part of their subculture. There were also the ramblers, campers and caravaners who combined together at weekends and on holidays to explore the countryside. This provided many opportunities for deep and reflective friendships. Where there is space and time for talk, friendships can grow and flourish.

As has been mentioned, there have been many social, economic and demographic changes in the second half of the twentieth century, which have changed the forms, styles and contexts of friendship. These include the decline and collapse of male-dominated heavy industries with their distinctive occupational sub-cultures. The massive growth of women's employment, particularly employment for married women, has done much to break down the distinctively gender-linked worlds of women in the home and men in the factory or office. Geographical and social mobility, the rapid expansion of higher education since the 1960s and the swift increase in divorce rates in the 1970s and 1980s all served in their distinctive ways to scatter the population. Increased affluence based on multiple-earner households encouraged people to move house as their material circumstances changed. In the 1980s and 1990s, the growth of a more flexible and insecure labour market was accompanied by increasing stress in the home. The perceived collapse of the psychological contract between employers and employees fuelled a real or imagined sense of insecurity that generated stress. Whether or not job turnover did actually increase is seemingly less relevant, for where people define situations as real, they are real in their consequences.

In what is perceived to be a more unstable and fluctuating world, men were less likely to expect to find close friends at work: the occupational communities had gone and increasing competition meant that colleagues at work became potential rivals. It would be dangerous to confide in a work colleague that one was feeling depressed or that there were domestic worries, if by doing so it demonstrated a weakness that might later be exploited. Women in part-time jobs were reluctant to jeopardize the advantages of having a job that suited them by joint gender solidarity against low rates of pay, insecurity, poor fringe benefits and all the other unsatisfactory aspects of part-time work. Survey evidence demonstrated that regular contact with family and friends declined from the mid-1980s to the mid-1990s. This was attributed partly to the pressures consequent upon the stressful juggling of family and work responsibilities, possibly now exacerbated by the physical problems of communication, with poor public transport and crowded roads.

Divorce and separation inevitably creates more complex and dispersed family links. Having responsibility for children from a former marriage and being physically separated or estranged from potentially supportive grandparents and other kin understandably makes people turn to friends. Individuals that stood by them at crucial turning points in their lives become particularly significant. Even if people are geographically separated, long telephone calls help to provide continuity. Now a younger generation may later keep in touch by e-mail when they have children.

With about a third of young people going on to higher education, a concept of friendship bonding has emerged, providing a source for close friends who may be part of a lifetime's personal community. Many readers of this book will have had the experience of meeting friends at university and coping with the problems of examinations, fluctuating relationships and sharing a house together. Learning to live on their own, away from family, forces young people to come to terms with who they are and how they want to live. Leaving college and seeking employment can be a very unsettling period and friends who supported them through their twenties are bonded with ties of gratitude and mutual experience. It may well be that for many it is sadness rather than joy that lays the foundation for long-lasting friendships. Friends who thought they were inseparable back-packing around the world return to follow their separate ways, while those who provide support when a parent dies, a partner leaves or when a good job crumbles are likely to be remembered for the rest of a person's life.

Those, then, who begin their adult lives in a reasonably non-competitive social world among peers are more likely to make long-lasting friends. School friends may fall by the wayside in adult life unless the lack of geographical mobility holds them together, or they remain, at least, as fossil friends. Job mobility among young adults, coupled with changes of residence, can lead to an inevitable revision of friendships and an acceptance of transitoriness in all their personal relationships. A number of failed relationships can lead to a re-evaluation of an earlier friend and same-sex friends can provide a greater continuity in the life-course for some people than their parents or partners.

It is important to remember that a number of individuals involved in friend-like relationships, whom adults may well refer to simply as 'friends', are more appropriately described as acquaintances. Such relationships do not depend on specific confidences or intimacies and are relatively superficial. As the social anthropologist Robert Paine has observed, acquaintances may portray a front of congeniality, which may be mandatory or a sensible precaution. Significantly, interactions between acquaintances change minimally when other persons join them. Most adults prefer to have acquaintances rather than friends at work: since they are the product of the situation, when a person leaves the job the relationship generally lapses. However, there are indications that it is only when a person has *left* a job that they are able to develop a true friendship with an earlier colleague. In one sociological analysis of friends at the workplace, it was observed that friendly relationships helped to control people in organizations by encouraging them to commit to the situation as it is, rather than withdrawing with a degree of alienation.

It is a commonplace to observe that there are friends and friends: fair-weather friends, heart-sink friends, dangerous friends, fossil friends – the potential for classifications and taxonomies are endless. Different styles of friendship have been distinguished: some echo family relationships, reflecting various degrees and types of dependency. Women may unconsciously have a mother-type friend to whom they turn for support and advice, or they may have a daughter-type relationship, so enjoying the admiration and liveliness of a younger woman. Men may be involved in similar father-son permutations. For both men and women mentor relationships at work can turn into long-standing relationships: this can be seen in industry, in the professions and in communal activities such as sports clubs or religious associations. This point will hardly need making to readers who have been juniors to a more senior advocate. One well-known contemporary example is the relationship between the British prime minister, Mr Blair, who was the junior to the man he appointed as lord chancellor – Lord Irvine. The two are said to be close friends. Of course the relationship can often be more appropriately described as one based on patronage and clientage. Such patron–client relationships develop in the academic world, where postgraduates are heavily dependent on their supervisors for references throughout their careers. However, long and lasting friendships can gradually lead to a reduction of dependency as the acolyte develops his or her own individual career and gains in status and experience thereby. The roles can then become reversed and distinguished professors be given opportunities by their former pupils, now in positions of power and responsibility. The Blair–Irvine example is by no means unique.

Other styles of friendship are reflections of previous or missing sibling relationships: a man who never had a brother, but was put down by elder sisters, may try to compensate for it in adult life. Once one has the idea, the permutations are endless. Some psychologists would argue that all friendships are echoes or reflections of classic family relationships. This needs to be seen in the context of changing patterns of relationships over the life-course. A man who may have unconsciously married his mother, or a woman who similarly has looked for a father substitute in her partner, may later seek friends outside the partnership which might reflect a longing for missed sibling relationships. The need for such a style of friendship could, in time, prove disruptive to the partnership.

Some would argue that the suffusing of what were once segregated gender roles in marriage with 'modern' confluent relationships based on companionship and friendship has shifted the emphasis away from commitment to choice. Traditional marriage was based on commitment 'in sickness and in health, 'til death us do part'. The relationships of late modernity, according to Anthony Giddens in *The Transformation of Intimacy*, are more likely to be based on choice and compatibility on a variety of dimensions. Thus, if the partner of one's youth does not fit the aspirations of middle age – or, to put it another way, if one has grown out of the need for a father figure – one may prefer to develop a confluent partnership with a brother figure. This tension between commitment and choice is at the heart of the dynamics of many people's personal communities. One of the most significant contemporary social trends could be that friendship is becoming more a matter of commitment.

This putative change, whereby certain chosen friends build up or acquire a degree of commitment that is kin-like in its quality, would carry with it many interesting social and sociological consequences. At present, the legal and bureaucratic boundary between kin and non-kin, however friendly the relationship may be, is sharp. Family law relates to relationships defined in a formal way. 'Next of kin' can be a designated friend, but confusions and difficulties can arise. For example, a man dying of AIDS might designate his friend-carer as next of kin, so that his parents visiting him in a hospice may not be given the privileged medical information they feel justified in claiming.

A 'modern' family-like style of friendship could be based on former lovers or partners. A relationship after a split may be such that the father of the children can, however exceptionally, continue to be a close friend of their mother, possibly established in a new relationship. Her new partner may not be so ready to encourage the friendship but this and similar scenarios are increasingly possible given the high incidence of divorce and its increasingly complex consequences.

Different styles of friendship would relate to whether the friend was readily accessible by living nearby or whether one's best friend was also a neighbour. Proximity allows a different style of intimacy from that of a friendship separated by the Atlantic Ocean, for example. Heterosexual friendships, couple friendships and the whole gamut of friendship styles pioneered and publicized by the Bloomsbury group are all part of the great range of possible relationships in the contemporary world of friendship. The topic deserves a longer and more extensive discussion than is possible here.

Friendship and gender

As part of the gender strife of the last twenty years, which has to some degree been reflected in academia by the growth of women's studies, there has been a concern to argue there are substantial differences between men and women with respect to the way in which they conduct their same-sex friendships. Traditionally, the position has been that friendship was primarily a masculine virtue. From the Old Testament to the ancient Greeks, it was male friendship that was extolled – with strong homoerotic overtones in the case of the latter. In 1969 Lionel Tiger published a book, *Men in Groups*, in which he claimed that men have a genetic predisposition, which is socially reinforced, to form enduring same-sex bonds. This socio-biological argument assumes that men's early experience as hunters and warriors encouraged them to co-operate as a means of survival. Women, not subject to such hazards, did not need, and hence did not inherit, the same bonding capacity.

In 1982 an article entitled 'Men's Friendships, Women's Friendships and the Alleged Inferiority of the Latter' was published in the American journal *Sex Roles*. At that time the editor, associate editors and book review editor were all women. The title of the article did not seem to appear contentious. The author, Paul Wright, claimed to have collected thousands of women's conversations over a period of more than ten years. An appreciable number of women expressed what they regarded to be an implicit understanding between women friends, namely, 'If two women have made arrangements to get together and one of them has an opportunity to get together with a man, the woman's date is automatically cancelled.' The overwhelming majority of men did not appear to have given the matter any thought.

In order to test these and other stereotypes, the writer attempted to define friendship in a very precise way and then – as is seemingly inevitable with social psychologists – set about testing samples of college undergraduates. The existing literature had already demonstrated that male friends tended to emphasize the commonality of shared activities and shared experiences, whereas female friends tended to emphasize reciprocity – helping, emotional support and confiding. As Wright remarked, 'Derogation of women's friendships seems to be much more common among the purveyors of conventional wisdom.'

The initial conclusions of this study are not particularly surprising: differences in men's and women's friendships did appear. These were consonant with traditional patterns of gender-differentiated roles and patterns of socialization, which defined women as more affective and socio-emotionally orientated and men as more instrumental and task-orientated. Their distinctive patterns of friendship were, in a phrase, context specific. However, perhaps of greater significance was the finding that the differences between women's and men's friendships diminished markedly as the strength and duration of the friendship increased. The author suggests that, with a broader sample base and continuing the study over a longer period of time, more similarity than dissimilarity in the way women and men conduct their friendships would appear.

The response from feminist writers who became interested in friendship was twofold. First, they argued that women's friendships were limited and restricted by patriarchy and capitalism, which produced differential power relations, making women subservient to men. Hence, as Pat O'Connor put it in her book *Friendships Between Women*, 'In a society where relationships with men are status enhancing and where women are defined as "the

Other", female friendships have a rather doubtful status – frequently seen as "going nowhere" and "a waste of time".' Women's friendships with each other did not seem to have direct access to power or status. However, a second strand of feminist writing sought to celebrate the more affective and caring side of women's friendships as being superior to what was disparagingly described as the 'inarticulate solidarity' of some men's friendships. Furthermore, women's friendships could be particularly significant and important to them, helping to affirm their separate identities and enabling them to become aware, in their distinctive forms of intimacy, that a new, different form of being was possible. The rhetoric of feminists such as the French psychologist Luce Irigaray carried visions of some kind of gender utopia based on a new awareness of womanhood, independent of male power and influence.

Evidently, this twofold response has inherent contradictions: it is hard to see how the oppressive patriarchal society produces the conditions for the emergence of a particularly liberating form of female friendship. Indeed, the reverse might be more plausible: as women embrace the values of contemporary market capitalism, so they become more free to choose their friends and to express themselves in multiple identities.

Feminists have, perhaps, been deluded by their own rhetoric and have failed to grasp that as the context changes, so too does the pattern and style of friendships. This change can take place in a very few months or even weeks. A very good example is provided by the miners' strike of 1984. Women in small, isolated, traditionally patriarchal mining villages were described as being socially oppressed and being limited to the social worlds of kin or chapel. However, as Dennis Warwick and Gary Littlejohn show in their book on Yorkshire mining villages, 'The women who had participated in support groups not only

reported being more conscious politically, they also said they were more self-confident and more socially aware.'

Clearly, such dramatic changes in economic circumstances and patterns of sociability should encourage caution in making too broad generalizations about putative links between gender and friendship. The contrast between the 'laddette' behaviour of the women in employment and the affective support of unemployed men has been well presented in the film *The Full Monty*, which had a remarkable resonance in Britain and the United States.

Some twenty years ago I did some research on friendship in a clothing factory on the Isle of Sheppey in Kent. All the workers were women and I detected a sharp break between the younger, unmarried women and the older women in their late forties and fifties. The younger ones, on a Monday morning, exchanged stories of their wild weekends of drinking, violence and sex, showing off their love bites and expressing with vivid obscenities how they saw off female rivals for their men, sometimes with the help of broken beer bottles. The older women, by contrast, were disapproving of such behaviour and spoke more of births, marriages and deaths and the composition and style of the ceremonies that marked them.

Another study, by Professor Beverley Skeggs of Manchester University, of ordinary – what might be called rather frumpy – stoutish working-class women, showed how their friendships helped to bond them and develop their self-esteem. They resented the way they felt demeaned at the cosmetic counters of department stores, for example, where hollow-cheeked over-made-up and possibly anorexic young women would attempt to freeze them away from using the scent samples. The source of oppression here is presumably a particular form of consumer culture that emphasizes youth and a body form quite impossible for most working-class women to achieve.

It is surely the case that any attempt to tie a particular form or style of friendship to men or women in general is a singularly fruitless exercise. At any particular socio-historical conjuncture it is certainly true that women may be more touchy-feely and men more inarticulate or stiff-upper-lipped. But, as I have suggested, styles can change very rapidly: some men can complain that they are doing all the emotion work as some women focus more on the labour market. Unquestionably, in recent years, women have done more caring and men have been 'less in touch with their emotions'. But all this can change very quickly. The British prime minister Mrs Thatcher set a style of tough and aggressive politics which fellow cabinet ministers, to be 'one of us', had to follow or be dismissed as 'wimps' and 'wets'. There is still a tendency to stereotype gender behaviour so that sensitive men are termed 'womanly' and tough women 'manly'. The stereotypes are crumbling. It is increasingly unhelpful to make these broad gender-based generalizations. Of course it is true, as our current empirical research at the University of Essex confirms, that women remain the key custodians of kin links and family-based sentiments and activities. But, having said that, I have published a study of a large and complex working-class family on the Isle of Sheppey in which one of the male siblings, a steel worker at the time, was universally described as 'the mother of the family'.

Within the limitations of given class and historical contexts there are interesting case studies of specific styles of friendship. One example, by the American sociologist Stacey Oliker, explored the best friends of married middle-class women in California. The way they talked with each other about motherhood and child-rearing helped to weave what she characterizes as a moral community. She argues that 'this flexibly-woven fabric of constraint constitutes a much more authoritative moral community than most "decline" theorists concede to modern life.' The moral discourse in which these women engage is about motherhood and family obligations and in some way undermines what Stacey calls 'the tyranny of expertise'. The close friendships between women help them to respect each other's individual liberty and attend to each other's welfare. Somehow their close friendships create a common dependency which encourages mutual responsibility, mutual independence and mutual agency.

Among Stacey's respondents, husbands seem less likely than friends to support their independent endeavours and ambitions. Their friends, however, are said to be more oriented to mutual self-development and autonomy and thus, perhaps unintentionally, often undermine their conjugal relationships.

This tension between partner and friends – one of the main themes of Oliker's book *Best Friends and Marriage* – is inevitably context specific. Furthermore, as with many sociological case studies based on modest samples, other case studies showing opposite or inconsistent results may be found. For example, Rosalind Coward in *Our Treacherous Hearts*, talked to 'almost 150' women, of which slightly over half were from the professional classes. She asserts, not entirely convincingly, that such an unbalanced sample may not necessarily invalidate her account, since 'some of the fears, pleasures and anxieties and pathologies which women currently experience in the family, seem to transcend the differences of race, class and region.' Coward, like Oliker, writes strongly within the feminist tradition and, also like Oliker, draws on the psychoanalytical writings of Jessica Benjamin. However, her interpretations are very different.

Rather than the 'vital community' of which Oliker so evidently approves, Coward records the feelings and anxieties of what she describes as guilty women. 'Guilt, guilt,

guilt. At one point I felt as though I would never hear about anything else.' Coward agrees with Oliker that women seem to suffer from the belief that achieving or doing things for themselves may be potentially damaging to other individuals. Thus, if they return to employment, their children may suffer or they won't have enough energy to be a good sexual partner. However, unlike Oliker's Californian women, the British women did not seem to find a solution to their problems in their friends. Indeed, competition more than co-operation seemed more likely. This is how Coward expresses it:

> many women, including myself, recognise that the friend-ships and networks centred on their children may also be their lifelines. But developing and maintaining real friend-ships and support around children is not an easy process. It is well worth it, but to achieve it sometimes involves women in facing and having to break through their old patterns of behaviour.
>
> To say this is to run counter to a prevailing ideology. Feminism is partly responsible for having peddled an ideal of female solidarity and friendship that would transcend hostile competitiveness, which was seen as largely a male characteristic. What was stressed was the common bond between women, rather than the rivalry. And although these views are no longer widespread as specifically femi-nist ideals, the notion still prevails that the automatic networking and support which women give each other in their shared work as mothers is founded on mutual identi-fication and love. Hostile and competitive feelings are supposed to be absent here.

Coward goes on to explore the actual hostility and com-petitiveness which women may feel for each other. This is a very personal and insightful analysis of great subtlety that goes well beyond our present concerns. She accuses women of complicity and of living an illusion and of not being able to sort out what comes from outside and what from within. Instead of recognizing who they are, Coward argues, they continue to project on to men and children what they haven't dealt with properly within themselves.

The idea that friends can be exploitative and a burden should not be overlooked. They invade space, take up time and generate guilt. Often those who may appear to be the sunniest, most sociable and charming 'friendly people' will confess that they long to escape from their friends. Greedy friends have been discussed since classical times, and it would be wise not to accept the somewhat smaltzy accounts of women's friendships, as a category, too readily. In a recent essay entitled *Women's Friendships in a Post Modern World*, Pat O'Connor suggests that friendships between women 'are still in some ways potentially at odds with a patriarchal culture'. However strong the qualifications, this statement should be received with caution: many friendships between men may also be at odds with a patriarchal culture. Surely the direction of *change* is of greater significance than the attempted maintenance of stereotypes.

I suggest that one of the reasons for the confusing and contradictory accounts of women's friendships *tout court* is that the nature and quality of friendship is changing in a very significant way. Rather than friendship being an alternative to family and kin links, there is a more fluid interchange of friend-like and family-like relationships. Hence, when Coward remarks that 'Buried emotions eventually erupt, jealousy, anger and competitiveness are often worse within and between families than in any workplace', it may be inferred that this judgement would not apply to friends. Yet as friends become closer and more salient for people's identities and serve as the focus for resolving some of their internal problems, so they, too, can become enmeshed in a complex emotional maelstrom. Women's friends have moved beyond being sources and recipients of chat and gossip or convenient members of a child support network. They may bring out deep and unresolved feelings of envy and guilt. Paradoxically, the fact that friends are becoming more family-like implies that they are not so easily dumped. There is an ongoing commitment based on the idea that too much has been invested to be able to withdraw without considerable loss to one's personal identity and sense of self. The friend who provides continuity through the loss of one's parents, the birth of one's children and, perhaps, a split up with one's partner is, simply, part of one's life. 'I know that she's always there for me' is a common phrase.

To some extent, it is true, some friends turn into myths, they are fossil friends who are rarely seen but serve as crucial markers in life's trajectory. They can turn into 'friends-in-the-mind' who may provide moral guidance and support even when not physically present. Such a fossil friend might continue even when deceased, since a true friend can exert influence by defining the social and moral limits of ego's behaviour. Asking oneself what so-and-so would have done or said in certain circumstances makes that other person still significantly present.

Perhaps we should be grateful that those feminists and others who have looked for a distinctive form of women's friendship have led us into these deeper waters. Simple social surveys that record how many 'friends' respondents may have, how often they see them and what they do with and for each other can sometimes suggest new ideas but more often they conceal more than they reveal. We return to this point in the next chapter.

The changing nature of adult friendship

Adult friendship seems an excessively slippery concept to pin down. It is complex, dynamic and context specific. Sociological and psychological writings can so readily slip into banalities. For example, an American psychologist concluded, 'The burdens of middle age leave little time for friendship.' This is surely an odd generalization to apply without qualification to all people in their forties and fifties in America. However, it is true that friendship requires time and material resources for it to flourish. Among the middle class, it may be argued, sociability is more likely to be planned and organized for its own sake, whereas working-class sociability may be more fortuitous. As Graham Allan astutely remarked, 'Because working class constructions of sociable relationships downplayed the significance of abstracted relationships in favour of context, the terminology of "friendship" often seemed to be inappropriate. Culturally, friendship involves an emphasis on the particularity of relationships over specific contexts of action.' In the working class it was – and in many areas still is – more appropriate to use the term 'mate', implying a different form of solidarity. The recognition of this distinction did much to explain why, in many surveys, working-class people reported fewer 'friends' than middle-class people.

Since some form of reciprocity invariably underlies friend-like relationships with non-kin, where material and social resources are limited, ways may have to be found for limiting the level of commitment. Thus men from different class backgrounds can meet regularly as drinkers in a pub, but relationships need not be extended to other spheres where social and economic differences would become explicit. Hence, an ethic of equality can be maintained in a ritualized drinking setting where limited reciprocities can be readily handled.

In general, if interaction can be limited to a particular setting focused on school, church, leisure and sporting activities, then episodes of interaction are relatively easy to control. It is a common experience for people to get to know each other in a particular context, for example, a choral society, and then for well-meaning people to suggest that there be more social occasions so that 'members can get to know each other better'. These events do not always achieve their purpose as people from different class-cultural backgrounds may perhaps find themselves sharing the same supper table. The awkwardnesses that may then emerge could later undermine the previous levels of friendly solidarity, based on the activity that brought everyone together, namely singing.

Allan's essay *Friendship and the Private Sphere* is a very useful corrective to the timeless and context-free differences in friendship patterns between men and women and working-class and middle-class people reported in many sociological studies. He reminds us that many working-class homes built in response to nineteenth century industrialization of inner-city areas were not physically suited for the entertainment of non-kin. The home was a private place and outsiders were not encouraged inside. This point is very well illustrated in a study of a Liverpool slum, *The People of Ship Street*, based on research by Madeline Kerr in the 1950s. She remarked how rare it was for people in this area to have adult friends, illustrating her point with the following vignette:

> Today Mrs Y, aged 72, told me she goes to the pub every evening for a glass of mild. She goes alone and returns alone. She is quite unafraid to do so even when it is dark. At the pub she meets her old friend Mrs X . . . and they sit

at the same table and have their mild together. These two ladies have known each other for 40 years yet they never make a change and have drinks in each other's homes for instance. They do not visit each other.

Similarly, in a sociological study carried out in the late 1940s in Coventry by Leo Kuper and others, a man who knew a neighbour at work in the factory was surprised to discover that he lived only a few doors away: 'I know him from work, but I didn't know he lived here. He doesn't drink – he's more of a man for his house. I have never seen him out.' This narrow confining of working-class patterns of non-kin relationships to specific settings is said by Allan to be an adaptive pattern arising out of the specific conditions of working-class life in such localities at a particular time. This argument is persuasive.

There is evidence, however, that in rural areas there was a different pattern. For example, in his classic study *Life in a Welsh Countryside*, based on fieldwork carried out in 1939 and 1940, Alwyn Rees remarks:

By friendliness towards his neighbours, the countryman overcomes the isolation imposed upon him by his environment. By welcoming them to his home, by visiting them in their turns, by helping them in their troubles and by co-operating with them in the performance of certain kinds of farm work, he maintains a form of society which dispenses with many of the functions of a central meeting place in a village or town. Offers of help arise naturally from companionship and, conversely co-operation promotes the growth of companionship and provides the occasion for its cultivation [. . .].

A favour can only be justified by friendliness, and friendliness means that one finds pleasure in the other's company and does not grudge spending time with him . . . Calculations would be alien to the spirit of friendliness, which pervades the whole system. After all, you cannot fully repay a neighbour who has helped you to harvest a crop under threatening clouds until you find him in similar difficulties.

A further significant point is that, in many studies of working-class communities up until the 1970s, couples were depicted as leading very segregated lives and their social links were unlikely to be jointly based. Men would perceive the home as their wife's preserve and would not consider bringing their own mates into it. Men and women's social activities were also more likely to be sharply compartmentalized. However, the trend over the last two decades of the twentieth century was for couples to lead much more integrated social and leisure lives. The enormous growth of package holidays encouraged couples to meet other like-minded couples, whom they may later decide to join in a foursome holiday.

Since couples are typically split between different work contexts and there may be certain inhibitions about becoming too friendly with neighbours, price-segregated package holidays provide a very convenient way of couples finding other couples who may progress to become close and supportive. The development of cross-sex friendships could, of course, be threatening, since the holiday context is notorious for loosening normative constraints. Again, this is a fertile soil for soap-opera scriptwriters and sociologists eager to undertake manageable case studies. The issue is not really how many couples meet other couples who later on become part of their personal support group in old age; rather, I suggest, it is that this is an example of a new context in which couple friends can be sampled and, possibly, recruited.

Friendship in later life

Friendship among the elderly is a topic of much significance to gerontologists. With the shift from residential to
'community' care over the past decades, it is clearly
important to have a 'community' to relate to. Typically,
the community has very often meant female relatives.
However, as kin links get geographically dispersed and
more women outlive their partners and siblings, so their
supportive friends come to have a considerable social
significance – almost as auxiliaries to the professionals
who have responsibility for health and social care. Such is
the significance of personal social support groups (PSSGs)
in old age that useful typologies have been devised,
enabling old people to be 'assessed' in terms of the type
of their PSSGs. Some are totally kin-based; others have
different mixes of close friends and responsible neighbours, with various permutations between them. Obviously, it is little help to an elderly person to have very
close friends at the other end of the country. A local
person who notices she has not drawn the curtains by
midday is of much greater importance.

Gerontologists are in agreement that friendship is of
great importance and value to the elderly. As partners and
relatives of the same generation die, friends, particularly
for the childless, come to have very great significance. Not
only can they serve obvious practical services, but they are
important for maintaining self-esteem and psychological
and social well-being. This is confirmed by recent research
by a team at Keele University: friends play an important
role in the networks of older people, often substituting for
a family where relatives are unavailable. Surprisingly, perhaps, neighbours appear less prominently in the personal
networks of older people.

In empirical research carried out in the United States, Sarah Matthews has shown how some people can manipulate their personal convoys so that they can have the social support of what they require when they need it. Her work involved obtaining life histories from her informants so that she could understand how their personal communities had emerged and could be restructured. She refers to one respondent who had acquired friends at each stage of life, and was able to draw on these dormant friends and, as it were, resurrect them in her old age. For this woman, friendships had accumulated through the years so that she now had a good selection from which to choose, obviously depending on the social situations of all concerned.

Dorothy Jerrome's anthropological research in Britain is probably the most subtle analysis of friendship among the elderly, based as it is on detailed ethnography. She focused particularly on women. While some were devastated by the lack of key relationships or unable to develop substitutes, others were able to enjoy active friendships for the first time. 'In old age, the life styles of never-married women and formerly married women with attenuated family ties converge, centring upon the activities of friendship.' In recognition of this, clubs for the elderly have been established to facilitate such friendships but, as Jerrome shows, the link between friendship and club membership is quite complex:

> An ideology of friendship and caring is expressed in formal gestures, in concern over illness, in the celebration of personal achievements and in the welcome extended in meetings. But friendship is a personal relationship involving intimacy, mutuality and shared leisure activities and is generally restricted to relationships founded outside the clubs and cutting across them. Club-going emerges as an

activity of friendship, the club providing a wider network into which pairs of friends may integrate.

Officially, the club has an ideology of the benefits of friendship and it is intended to serve as a means for introducing people to potential friends and to consolidate the bonds of friendships. The organizers are committed to creating 'a friendly club', but some of their attempts at social engineering have been counter-productive. One example from Jerrome's rich and subtle study will have to serve, and it demonstrates that a carefully observed and documented study such as this can be far more revealing and valuable than many larger-scale and quantitative studies. It is a model of its kind.

The tension between personal needs for intimacy and the organisational aims of a friendly club surfaces in different ways. It is the basis of arguments about seating. The executive committee of the Good Companions Club have struggled for years to build up the membership. They are baffled by the failure of their friendly atmosphere and lively programme to gain new members. The problem lies in the seating arrangement itself. The circle of chairs was too intimate and too public. Unless it is whispered to a next door neighbour, everyone is party to a conversation. Inadvertently establishing eye contact with someone on the opposite side requires acknowledgement, but the rules governing this kind of communication are uncertain. Unable to slip in at the back, the newcomer also feels exposed.

Ironically, the organisers' insistence on free access to seats in the name of friendship ultimately defeats the goal of integrating the newcomer, as the following case shows. Miss C doesn't feel she really belongs to the Sunday Club. She had originally been invited by a friend but got there before her. She was turned away from two tables where the empty seats had already been reserved and finally went home. On the way she met her friend who had later told the organiser what had happened. The organiser was angry with the members of the two offending tables and ordered Miss C to move from table to table in future. Miss C, a shy and unassertive woman, obeys, but has no real friends in the club: she drifts in and out permanently on the margin of things. Women like Miss C are in the minority, even in this club set up by a charitable organisation specifically for lonely people (defined by the organisers as those living alone). A preponderance of people with her needs would, in fact, make the club unviable. Participation in the social club populated by people as lonely as each other is an unrewarding experience which contributes to the low success rate of such organisations. In a sense, women like Miss C are ineligible for friendship, even in a friendship club (set up to help isolated people make friends). The very fact of membership in a club for lonely people makes them unattractive to each other for it reveals their own need for friends and lack of success in making such relationships by conventional means. Club members know too much about each other for comfort: they are too much alike each other to help each other. Membership of a friendship club is itself a demoralising experience, and admission of social failure. In interaction with others, the lonely woman's low self-esteem is reinforced by seeing herself reflected in those around her: unattached, ageing and lonely in a society which values youthfulness and family life, where value is attached to sociability, and where social life is couple-orientated. Lacking in confidence and unpractised in the skill of self-presentation, the lonely woman finds the unstructured setting of the social club for unattached people, where there are few prescriptions for behaviour and where first contacts are hindered by the knowledge that she is being assessed as a potential friend, especially daunting. The Sunday Club is officially for the socially isolated older person, but it is in fact dominated by women who are socially active and well connected. Miss C provides an exception. But her experience confirms the point that if the club were just for really lonely people like her and attracted no others, it would be a failure.

Another piece of empirical research carried out in the United States, by Rebecca Adams and Rosemary Blieszner, attempted to discover whether those structurally advantaged early in life were better placed to have good, supportive friends in old age. Not unreasonably it might be assumed that those more financially secure, with higher levels of education, would have more means and opportunities to acquire and retain friends. Those rich in cultural capital are more likely to accumulate social capital, as the current jargon has it. Those assessing elderly people and perceiving the signs of cultural capital – books, CDs, etc – in the home and meeting an articulate, well-educated person might well imagine that these are valid indications that such a person would be less likely to need public support. Furthermore, if such people were found to have problematic friendships, perhaps too close or demanding or just fading away, such friendships could readily be replaced by their superior social skills and networking capacities.

The study was carried out in Greensboro, North Carolina in 1990 and was based on twenty-eight women and twenty-five men aged between fifty-five and eighty-four years. These respondents acknowledged various degrees of 'problematic' friendships, since half of them mentioned a friendship that was 'difficult' and two-thirds reported one that was 'fading away'. Much to the researchers' surprise, the results of their study were directly counter to their initial expectations. Problematic friendships were actually more likely among the 'young-old', financially better-off women or those in the upper middle class. These would seem to be the very people that, on the face

of it, one would expect to be securely socially bonded.
Women are conventionally perceived to be better 'friend-
makers', and *a fortiori* this would apply to those in the
more financially secure upper middle class.

Once the researchers had their counter-intuitive results,
they were obliged to devise some new hypotheses. Maybe
those who have always been able to make friends easily
were more able to dump problematic friends, believing
that they would be easily replaced. Perhaps the culturally
advantaged have higher expectations of friendship, and
because of the strength of their own resources they have
preferred to let old friends fade away rather than get
entangled in emotionally exhausting relationship work.
Such a cynical supposition would suggest that perhaps the
structurally privileged elderly in Greensboro are not particularly amiable people. Alternatively, the authors suggest, the friend dumpers may just be more honest and
confident and the lower-middle class respondents more
mealy-mouthed (that is not precisely how the authors put
it, but they were writing in a scholarly journal). The
authors recognize that their research is problematic for
those concerned with social policy or what they call 'individual or group intervention' (i.e. social engineering)
'aimed at both those with few friends and those with
problematic relationships'.

This article may be symptomatic of an emerging mana-
gerial social science, which feels impelled to move on from
attempting to understand what is to prescribing what
ought to be. Even if social scientists agree with their
colleagues in private that they hold to the spirit of Max
Weber's discussion of values and objectivity, they may still
feel obliged to collude with professional social fixers, if
only to ensure funding for their research. The authors
suggest two possibly useful programmes arising out of
their research: the first would be designed 'to help struc-

turally disadvantaged people articulate problems in their relationships' (i.e. stop the poor and insecure being so mealy-mouthed) 'and create opportunities for finding new friends' (i.e. go out and smile to get someone to do your shopping for you). The second programme would be to help the structurally advantaged people 'to make decisions regarding the acquisition, repair and termination of friends' (i.e. don't dump your friends dear, you never know when you may need them). The authors conclude by recognizing that having more friends does not necessarily imply that an elderly person receives more social support. It may equally imply that such a person has more worries and relationship problems.

This section on the importance of friendship for the elderly has not done justice to a rich and rapidly growing literature, since the importance of the issue does not have to be justified to practitioners, who are eager to support academic research on the issue. Scholarly studies such as those by Dorothy Jerrome make clear the complexities and subtleties involved in social intervention. It would be easy to mock the well-intentioned purposes of club organizers and gerontologists. In the same way that some elderly people need advice about diet or exercise, so some need help and support in generating and maintaining friends. There is a clear need not simply for well-intentioned social workers and club organizers, but for social scientists who may not be thanked for showing that social life is highly complex. However, it is not random, as the work of George Homans, in his *Social Behaviour*, has shown. Perhaps practitioners would be better prepared if they were taught more rigorous social theory in their training programmes. This might deter many worthy people who want to bustle on in a helpful way. However, as Dorothy Jerrome and others have shown, their admirable enthusiasm may, in the end, be unproductive.

Conclusion

Despite the very large literature generated by developmental and social psychologists in the second half of the twentieth century, it does appear, happily, that friendship has successfully eluded their grasp. It would be so convenient for them if having many friends was a clear indicator of achievement. However, they have had to concede, as we have seen many times in this chapter, that, for many of the problems they wish to study, it is the quality of the relationship that matters. Friendship, more perhaps than any other aspect of our social lives, has eluded the attempts of social scientists to be classified and codified. Sociologists, too, are now much more wary about playing their traditionally strongest cards of class and gender and are coming to acknowledge the fluidity, if not the slipperiness of contemporary styles of friendship and the need to place these styles in context.

Certainly friendship does change through the life-course, but echoes of previous styles can re-emerge. Divorce and remarriage can re-create the self-centred relationship-obsessed style of the twenty or thirty somethings a quarter of a century later on in life. The caring friendships of the elderly can be found among those supporting friends dying of AIDS or cancer much earlier in life. Attempts to describe a 'normal' lifetime friendship trajectory inevitably flounder into banalities. With that warning we can now turn, in the final chapter, to consider the practical and political advantages and disadvantages of focusing on the usefulness of friendship.

5

Social Capital and the Politics of Friendship

Those, who liked one other so well as to joyn into Society, cannot be but supposed to have some Acquaintance and Friendship together, and some Trust one in another.

John Locke, *Second Treatise on Government*

Individualism is a mature and calm feeling, which disposes each member of the community to sever himself from the mass of his fellows and to draw apart from his family and friends, so that after he has formed a little circle of his own, he willingly leaves society at large to itself.

Alexis de Tocqueville, *Democracy in America*

Early in 1999 the well-known British TV presenter and personality Sheena McDonald suffered an extremely serious road accident. She was unconscious for seventy-two hours and in intensive care for two weeks. Some thought that she would not survive. Seven months later she wrote about her experiences:

Having more or less lived for work, I now followed the cliched path common to many survivors of accident or illness. I now consider friends and family to be far more important.

Later on, she adds that she has 'stared death in the face and lived to tell the tale (with a lot of help from my friends, in my case).'

There is now a substantial and growing amount of evidence to show that social support can protect people from the worst consequences of a variety of pathological states from arthritis through tuberculosis to depression. Social support can be deconstructed into different aspects: subjects are better supported if they are cared for and loved, that they are esteemed and valued and that they believe that they belong to a network of communication and mutual obligation. In a very early study among soldiers during the Normandy campaign of World War II, it was found that every soldier who lost 75 per cent or more of his comrades suffered combat exhaustion.

Since this early research, the results of which are not altogether surprising, a number of very thorough epidemiological studies have been carried out. The results published in medical journals are rigorously scientific and authors rightly make sharp distinctions between co-relations and causation. A paper in the *Journal of the Medical Association* in 1997 demonstrated convincingly that more diverse social networks were associated with greater resistance to upper respiratory illness (i.e. colds). The cautious introduction to the paper is worth quoting at some length to illustrate the complexity of the research problem:

> The hypothesis that multiple ties to friends, family, work and community are beneficial in terms of physical health has gained substantial support over the last decade. Particularly provocative is epidemiological evidence that those who participate in more diversified social networks – for example, are married, interact with family members, friends, neighbours and fellow workers, and belong to social and religious groups – live longer than their counter-

parts with fewer types of social relationships. This association has been reported in multiple prospective studies, and *the relative risk for mortality among those with less diverse networks is comparable in magnitude to the relation between smoking and mortality from all causes* [my italics]. Unfortunately, the behavioural and biological characteristics that link social networks of greater scope to longevity have not been identified.

The author goes on to report that greater network diversity has also been associated with less anxiety, depression and non-specific psychological distress.

It is not appropriate here to explore this and other similar technical papers in detail. Suffice it to say that there is a growing interest and concern with what I prefer to call personal communities, rather than social networks, for the reasons mentioned in the Introduction (pages 6–8 above). The problem, of course, is to understand the precise mechanisms that link lack of social support with various adverse medical conditions. For example, there is plenty of evidence to show that separated and divorced people suffer more acute and chronic illnesses that limit their daily activities than do married people. Separated and divorced individuals have significantly greater mortality from certain diseases, including pneumonia, tuberculosis, heart disease, and some types of cancer. It is suggested that immunological changes associated with psychological distress may increase one's susceptibility to infectious disease and perhaps cancer.

Forms and styles of social support

At certain times, there may be various problems and tensions *within* one's personal community that add hugely to one's psychological distress. Just as there are friends and friends, so there are different types and styles of personal communities. Clearly, an important research frontier would be to focus more sharply on the dynamics of personal communities and how they may be changing as a result of the demographic, social and economic forces in contemporary society. If the internal balance of personal communities between family and friends is changing – and evidence is accumulating that indeed it is – then the full implications of such a putative shift need to be carefully considered. There has to be a focus on the qualitative nature of different forms and styles of personal communities: individuals are more likely to feel loved, esteemed, valued and in a mutually supportive micro-community of social connectedness in some forms of personal community rather than in others. While there is clear evidence that those who are most socially isolated are at an increased mortality risk from a number of causes, there is also evidence that *certain types of social support are more effective than others*. Close confidants are more significant than looser acquaintances or trophy friends. There is also some indication that relationships with friends can be more important than relationships with kin in the recovery from certain conditions. More research is needed to discover why this might be so. It is possible that Aristotle's friend of virtue is of the greatest help, since such a person, as another self, is more likely to be sharply focused on their friend and is thus particularly well qualified to observe and understand the nuances of their behaviour. One might expect parents or partners to have the same quality of care and awareness, but if parents are seen infrequently and the partner is overstressed with work, they may not have the time and emotional energy to provide the gentle, supportive friendship that is required.

Aristotle's friends of pleasure and utility, by contrast, may be part of one's personal community but may be quite disfunctional in health terms. In a review of these issues, Toni Antonucci and Kees Knipscheer ruefully remark, 'if network members smoke, drink, take drugs, engage in unhealthy or excessive eating habits, it is both less likely that individuals will attempt to change that behaviour in themselves or that they will be able to sustain that change in behaviour over the long term.' Going round to one's friends to borrow the proverbial cup of sugar may not be doing one's health much good.

While there is a growing body of medical opinion that recognizes the importance of social support as a moderator of life stress, it is not at all clear what precise *processes* are being reflected in such an observation. What does the support of close friends or relatives precisely mean? In the case of those with more cultural capital, their personal communities are likely to include those with specific skills as doctors, lawyers, counsellors or even psychoanalysts. A number of studies have supported the hypothesis that individuals of higher socio-economic status are more likely to have friends with money, education and training upon which they can draw in a crisis.

Other studies have emphasized the importance of having one particular confidant, and it seems that women are more likely to have these than men. Men might use their partners in this way, but those who don't or can't may find that their personal communities of friends of pleasure and utility are ill-equipped to deal with emotional or medical crises.

Some readers may well be surprised that researchers should be so painstaking in discovering what they might consider to be obvious. It surely must be the *quality* of the relationship with significant others that is the basis for the most effective social support. Returning to the analogy of social capital, there are solid investments that steadily accumulate, and there is liquid capital available for any emergency. But there are also investments that fail. Other forms of capital have restricted access that make them unavailable, perhaps, when most needed. Similarly, the various ingredients of personal communities, an important element of social capital, have to be unpacked. The importance of various types of relationship varies as a function of the age, sex-role identification, marital status, and socio-economic status of the individuals involved. It is not friendship *per se* that is important, but rather the trust, security, feelings of self-esteem and feelings of being loved for one's own sake which may flow from it. Hence, it is now recognized that research needs to be focused on the essential nature of the close communicating friendship. One review of the practical importance of friendship by John Goffman and Jeffrey Parker, two American psychologists, concluded:

> Even if the discussion of personal matters is a general criterion of an intimate relationship, this leaves a great deal unknown. What kind of information is disclosed, at what level of intimacy, and how does this come about? Also, what is the response to the disclosure? Is it problem solving, nurturance, empathy, reciprocal disclosure or engagement in various activities together? *Dyadic social processes have not been examined* [my emphasis].

This final sentence is surely an exaggeration, given the years of research on marriage and spousal dynamics. However, it again reflects what we found in the last chapter, namely a dearth of studies exploring qualitative aspects of intimacy outside a marriage partnership. In particular, there needs to be research which focuses on whether other members of a personal community can provide an adequate substitute for a strong supportive relationship with a spouse. Basic descriptive research on what friends actually talk about or do together is scarce.

When considering the quality and efficacy of social support, as illustrated by interactions in personal communities, it is important to remember that a description of an individual's personal community at any one point of time is a snapshot. Some individuals will have greater depth or offer greater return in terms of social capital if they have been part of an individual's personal community, as developed over the lifespan. This is what I have referred to as a social convoy. Someone who has experienced a bereavement, for example, and has been effectively comforted by a friend, may carry latent reciprocal support through a lifetime. The accumulation of supporting experiences of various forms eventually leads individuals to feel securely that they are capable and competent people and that they can be confident in knowing that there are significant others who believe in them, who love them and who can be counted on in a crisis. Having this social support empowers people to live more effectively and, indeed, more healthily and for longer.

So far we have been considering the practical effects of social support in buffering the effects of social stress and in recovering from various adverse health conditions. The message is clear: anyone with heart problems, for example, who has never been married, who lives alone and who lacks social support has a substantially greater risk of dying earlier and less chance of a good recovery from myocardial infarction. However, friends have other uses. In some pioneering work at the University of Essex Institute for Social and Economic Research, Carmel Hannan was able to demonstrate the crucial importance of friends in helping people to exit from unemployment.

Hannan builds on the work of the American sociologist Mark Granovetter, whose work on finding jobs is relatively unsophisticated. Granovetter assumed that the amount of time two people spent together could be taken as a proxy for the closeness of the relationship. However, people clearly have many good friends they do not see regularly. Indeed, data from the British Household Panel Study (BHPS), which is based on a large, national sample, showed that 20 per cent of people contacted their best friend only once a month or less frequently. Hannan recognizes the importance of judging the nature of friendship according to criteria internal to the character of the given relationship. Rather than getting surrogate measures of closeness (e.g. frequency of contact) Hannan argues that it is better to allow respondents to define their close relationships for themselves, even though the criteria they use are not necessarily specified. She therefore used those named by the respondents as their three closest friends for the purposes of her analysis. Since she was using survey data, she had no means of unpacking the actual relationship to consider the importance of trust and mutually reciprocal obligations. Hannan's analysis involved highly sophisticated statistical analyses in order to assess the relative importance of a whole string of factors that might be hypothesized as bearing upon the probability of entering employment from unemployment. Her robust conclusion still remained: that it was the employed *close* friends of unemployed people who played the strongest role in determining unemployment exit rates. This is a striking amendment to Granovetter's position, which emphasized those friends to whom his respondent had relatively weak ties.

Evidence from the BHPS shows that 60 per cent of unemployed men in the sample reported asking friends and other contacts in their personal communities when looking for jobs. It does appear that these play an important role. However, it would be wrong to jump to a naïve form of social engineering so that unemployed people are introduced to buddies who are employed, because Hannan also showed that those unemployed men who have employed close friends suffer more psychological stress, as measured by the General Health Questionnaire (GHQ). Presumably their employed friends put social pressure upon them, whereas if unemployed people's friends are also unemployed, the putative psychological stress is alleviated. Evidently, some kind of balance needs to be struck, since friends in employment do provide information and aid in finding a job. It may well still be the case that more distant friends are effective in finding employment, since they are likely to work in different labour markets for different employers. The Hannan–Granovetter debate will continue!

Personal communities as social capital

This example leads nicely into a consideration of one of the paradoxes that emerges when the idea of social capital, mentioned in the Introduction, is unpacked and the importance of friendship is revealed. A recent study by the English Health Education Authority, *Social Capital and Health*, attempted to operationalize the rather general formulations of social capital put forward by Robert Putman in his recent writings in America. The author's conclusions are significant:

> This report highlights Putman's neglect of . . . small-scale often geographically micro-level, informal networks of friends, neighbours and relatives, which our data suggest are the major source of social capital available to members of local English communities.

This being so, it cannot be assumed that these micro-social worlds are all too ready to be harnessed to the current government's programme, however benign and beneficial this may appear to be. Personal communities can be inward-looking, conservative, resistant to change and easily mobilized as subversive or possibly criminal elements in society.

In the United States, Herbert J. Gans has come to similar conclusions in his study of *Middle American Individualism*, where he emphasizes the importance of micro-social worlds. He recognizes, returning to our term, that in personal communities 'People invite, choose and exclude, so that associates tend to be like-minded and fairly homogenous in some traits and major interests. In the absence of formal rules, the major regulating devices are mutual trust, reciprocity, gossip and social pressure, and banishment if nothing else works.' Clearly, some people *will* be excluded and loneliness and isolation may follow. This is, perhaps, the dark side of friendship about which little has been written. The more the idea of friendship is discussed, the more those who define themselves as deficient in friends may feel deprived and excluded.

Gans is to some extent providing a counter-polemic to that put forward in *Habits of the Heart* by Robert Bellah and others (see above, page 4). He remarks that American society, and people's image of it, is dominated by large, formal organizations. The more they grow, the more people need their own havens, which makes Gans believe that informal groups may be more important now than in the past. However, there is a danger that informal groups will be romanticized and seen as a social glue of unequivocal benefit to society. In the same way in which friends can support bad habits and antisocial behaviour, so, 'informal groups are often exclusionary, and relations inside them can be competitive, manipulative and conflict driven.'

Social capital is by no means an unmixed blessing. Friends evidently adopt criteria of preference that are highly particularistic. Philosophers have considered with high moral seriousness whether, when faced with the prospect of two people drowning, for example, it is morally right to save one's friend rather than the other person. The conclusion seems to be that it is, but that applies only in the private sphere: it is not morally permissible to bend the rules of formal organization in the public sphere to benefit one's friends.

But, of course, friends do look after each other. Friends of utility who are well placed gain power, influence and money with the help of their friends. The more complex the rules and regulations, the more having a good contact is necessary to make sure that files are not 'lost', 'mislaid', or whatever.

Social capital in the former Soviet Union and China

Friendship played a particularly important part in the former Soviet Union. Friends in Soviet society characteristically maintained very intense contact, frequently meeting every day. According to one Soviet study, 16 per cent of people met their friends every day, 10 per cent two or three times a week and 22 per cent weekly. Given that the essence of friendship is the rejection of the idea of intervention or control by any third party, it could be seen as subversive to the collective values of the society. In theory, there was no place for friendship in Soviet ideology. As George Orwell and others recognized, friendship is an obstacle to the absolute domination of the state over the individual. Friendship frequently constitutes the basis for the creation of underground organizations and anti-governmental activities. Crucially, friends trust each other, and certain kinds of information can only flow between friends. In the former Soviet Union, friends as soul-mates, Aristotle's friends of virtue, were vital in maintaining a sense of personal integrity in a society where the façade was more important than the reality.

Friendship had hugely practical importance under the old Soviet regime. In the words of Vladimir Shlapentokh, in his fascinating book *Public and Private Life of the Soviet People*:

> Soviet people provide each other with considerable assistance in 'beating the system'. Friends play an extremely vital role in procuring necessary goods, for they constantly buy each other food, clothing, shoes, or other items, should the chance arise, i.e., should these items appear in stalls. Even more important is the assistance of a friend who has access to closed stores or cafeterias. It is considered perfectly ethical for people to ask their more privileged friends to bring food or clothes from places that are generally inaccessible to them.
>
> Friends are extraordinarily active in providing other assistance in everyday life. They help their friends find a job, place children in a good high school or college, or get into a hospital or health resort. The importance of friends is directly proportional to the unavailability of goods or services, and is inversely proportional to the importance of money in obtaining hard to find items . . . The obligations of friendship, as well as those of the family, also tend to undermine objectivity in public life. For example, professional performance, which should ideally be the only guide for the distribution of rewards in a society striving for efficiency and justice, may become subordinate to access based on whom one knows.

Furthermore, this great focus on friends in Soviet society was undoubtedly a very important manifestation of social capital maintaining social cohesion. Beyond the level of the best friend, or *droog*, was a whole network of acquaintances, providing connections to dozens of offices and enterprises throughout the country. The really close friends simply could not provide this extensive benefit system:

> The friends of friends as well as the acquaintances of friends, turn the whole of Soviet society into closely interwoven networks, where there are only one or two individuals between you and an official or sales person whose favour you need.
>
> Friends of friends, unlike acquaintances, are not always people the individual meets regularly. Contact with them is usually only through communication with the common friend or at certain occasions, for instance, at birthday parties. However, people recognise that the bonds of friendship are such that friends of friends can be immediately mobilised to assist a person who is their common friend.
>
> The contingent of acquaintances is recruited differently to that of friends. Since trust is a main criterion in selecting friends, Soviet people prefer to have as friends those they know from childhood or at least from their university or college. Forty per cent of the friendships of the respondents of one survey began in high schools or other schools. Acquaintances, however, are found mostly at the workplace, or in resort places, on tourist trips, and at meetings and conferences.

It is possible that many Soviet people consciously or unconsciously misinterpreted friendship as being synonymous with 'comradeship' and collectivism, so that its truly subversive nature was hidden through a process of cognitive dissonance. It was normal practice, in what was for many years considered a world superpower, for anyone who had access to any resources to use them to satisfy their own needs first. No one should be surprised that a large proportion of the billions of dollars provided by the International Monetary Fund should have recently been siphoned off by individuals into Swiss bank accounts and into various systems of money laundering.

I have emphasized the importance of friends and friendship in the former Soviet Union to illustrate the point that the development of society based on friendship is not necessarily to be welcomed. Yet anyone from the West who was able to visit the Soviet Union in the bleak Brezhnev years for any length of time was deeply impressed by the overwhelming friendship and hospitality expressed in the so-called kitchen-culture. The conviviality and warmth invariably found there was in marked contrast to the stultifying formality and hypocrisy of public life.

Friendship also plays an important part in contemporary Eastern societies. In China the personal connections known as *guanxi* play an important part in its business culture. Given that China may well be one of the world's four largest economies by 2010, it would seem important for Western societies to understand the significance of *guanxi* network building. In a survey of 2000 Chinese from Shanghai, 92 per cent recognized the importance of *guanxi* in their lives and 72 per cent preferred to use *guanxi* connections over normal bureaucratic channels to advance personal interests. Significantly, younger respondents put a greater emphasis on *guanxi* than older people. As in the Soviet Union, the communist ideology and dominating state control did much to encourage the reaction of people retreating to the social support and the security of their own private spheres of *guanxi* networks. Recent research on business executives suggests that building strong *guanxi* relations with the right persons is crucial to the attainment of long-term business success in China. Developing these connections takes much time and care. Most *guanxi* is based on kinship. Locality is also important. Achieving *guanxi* for non-Chinese investors is not easy. An intermediary who is a mutual friend of both is essential: who you know is worth much more than what you know. Personal references count more than simple financial inducements. However, also of great importance are tendering favours (i.e. straight bribes such as sponsoring and supporting the children of Chinese officials at universities abroad), nurturing mutual advantages, cultivating a personal interest in the business partner by sharing inner feelings and personal secrets and, perhaps most importantly, cultivating trust. Such strategies for building and maintaining *guanxi* reflect the five fundamental dimensions of it, namely, instrumentalism, personal relationships, trust, reciprocity and longevity. Irene Yeung and Rosalie Tung claim that:

Under the influence of Confucianism these societies share the following characteristics: disdain for institutional law; strong bonds on the basis of blood, ancestral village, and school and military ties; a clear demarcation between members of the in- versus out-groups; an inability to grasp the interdependent relationship of situations that may not be obvious to westerners; a tendency to view matters from a long-term perspective. These characteristics contribute to the significance of connections in virtually all social functions, business being one of them. While relationships of networking are also important in the West, their role is often overshadowed by institutional law, which establishes what can and should be done.

The authors believe that attempts by governments to replace the importance of connections by institutional law will fail, since that would be to undermine very deep and fundamental values in Confucian societies. Even if their position is overstated, the role of the *guanxi* cannot be ignored.

The ambiguous relationship between social capital and social exclusion

Given the putative difficulties posed by *guanxi* in the globalization of American corporate culture, it is perhaps surprising that many Western governments should now be looking favourably on informal social ties in their own societies as the basis for reducing social exclusion. Lumping together social networks, personal communities and other forms and styles of social connectedness under the umbrella of social capital, government policy advisors are rapidly learning the sociological fundamentals put forward by Georg Simmel and Émile Durkheim. Notwithstanding Durkheim's self-confessed failure to find the secret of social cohesion in order to avoid the *anomie* inherent in industrial-capitalist society, the new social fixers busily put their minds to the building of social capital. Thus, in Britain, the influential think tank DEMOS, whose first director became a senior advisor to the chancellor of the exchequer, published a report entitled *The Wealth and Poverty of Networks*. In this report it was suggested that people – implicitly, of course, working-class people – could have the 'wrong' social networks: 'Those people whose networks are dominated by strong ties to family, neighbours, old school friends and people like themselves, have fewer chances to find work and fewer chances of mobility.' (Tell that to an old Etonian!) Indeed, such a conclusion could well be one implication of Carmel Hannan's research mentioned above. The author of the DEMOS article concludes:

Governments should be enabling people to develop and use their networks. At the very least, it should stop reinforcing the wrong kind of networks . . . Placing unemployed people in a training room where they only meet other unemployed people much like themselves does nothing for their networks.

It is not enough to give people money or skills. 'Just as the élite get on because of who they know as well as what they know, so do the life chances of the socially excluded depend on their contacts.'

The anthropologist Mary Douglas, in the same DEMOS report, poses a crucial question:

Should public policy encourage a society of weak ties, supporting greater mobility and change? Or should it try to foster a culture of long-term commitments? . . . Strong ties are best for certain dependent categories of the population such as infants, elderly people, the handicapped and the chronically infirm. But strong ties broken are hard to mend: it is not easy to foster them at the right phase in the life cycle and to loosen them at other times. Weak ties on the other hand, appeal to our cultural bias in favour of an open society.

Mary Douglas has, I suspect, dampened the enthusiasm of those who want to unpack social capital into benign social networks and 'weak ties'. The amount of social engineering involved in manipulating social-tie strengths through the life-course could be daunting, even for the most control-obsessed government. Happily, the relationship between social capital and social exclusion is so ambiguous that in a few years a new fad will hit policy-makers as someone does another repackaging of long-established sociological processes.

As Alejandro Portes very effectively remarked, in a

much-quoted review of social capital 'Communitarian advocacy is a legitimate political stance; it is not good social science.' That applies to much of the concern to harness social capital to specific policy ends.

The politics of friendship

It is time to return to Aristotle. All friendship presupposes a form of community – the term personal community has been extensively used in this book. It follows that the general well-being of a community will depend on the extent of the friendly feelings that its members share. For Aristotle, friendship in communities implies advantage and therefore civic or political friendship must be a variety of the friendship of utility. So, let us be clear, political friendship cannot be a primary friendship, although civic friends might try to claim that they are enjoying a moral friendship. Aristotle is highly sceptical, if not cynical. Nevertheless, he does accept that, 'If people are friends, they have not need of justice.'

One might have expected Aristotle to be more enthusiastic about political friendship and even to have some advice for those ruling the state as to how friendship among the citizenry can best be promoted. It would seem to be self-evidently true that a friendly society would be a good society. However, Aristotle appears to argue that it is not the quality of friendship that creates civic virtue, but rather it is the constitution of the state which largely determines both the nature and extent of the civic bond and its moral worth. Civic friendship will therefore vary according to the constitution of the state in question. As any existing actual polity is sure to be inferior to Aristotle's perfect constitution, so civic friendship falls short of primary friendship. Somewhat gloomily, Aristotle suggests that democracies are too unstable to make the formation and cultivation of civic friendship possible. Citizens are often deeply divided ideologically and, as we saw in the case of Sue in Chapter 3, friendship can rarely hold two people together when there is a fundamental clash of values.

At the risk of some repetition, I now conclude this chapter by relating Aristotle's friendship of virtue to the ideal of a friendly society. We have already noticed that friendship could be seen as a threat to the smooth and harmonious functioning of the social order, since friends and lovers may withdraw emotional energy from a wide range of institutional roles and relationships. As a number of observers have noted, all deep loves and friendships are thus akin to a form of regression from higher levels of social organization.

Societies respond to this potential threat to social institutions either by seeing friendship as a private matter for individuals in which the state takes no interest or by attempting to incorporate friendship, albeit in a weaker form, into its own institutions.

However, whether friendship is perceived to be a matter that is primarily private or partially public, it cannot but have political implications. First, friendship can be dangerous and disruptive. In political purges of all types to be a friend of a victim is a highly dangerous position to be in. Stalin's victims were often under horrifying pressure to betray their friends. Family connections could be readily discovered: true friends were potentially more dangerous but also more easily hidden. A traditional Russian fable describes a captive prince's willingness to sacrifice wives, children and retainers, all of whom could be replaced, but when, by chance, the victor slaughters the captive prince's friend, the prince breaks down in anguish. Persecutors are quite often right: conspiracies are frequently organized around the ideals of friendship. Partners in crime make strong partners, the status of an outlaw providing a strong impetus for the formation of friendships.

A second political implication of friendship is that it is fundamentally egalitarian, and one of the strongest barriers to pure friendship is structurally conditioned inequality. One good measure of the existence of a class-stratified society is the empirical existence of structural divisions or faults reflecting the normative, relational and economic aspects of class. Friendship links that cross putative class boundaries would serve to undermine arguments based on the immutability of given class structures. Typically, strong pressures exist in class-structured societies to avoid the formation of friendships between social unequals. This may, for example, involve the normatively sanctioned rules of exclusion and inclusion, such as those determined by parents for their children or rigidly segregated eating arrangements within institutions and organizations. Rules of social distance are rigidly practised at the top of British monarchical society, and there are reflections of this throughout the complete social structure. A truly friendly society would, of course, be a classless society, and so, logically, giving a greater centrality and salience to pure friendship could be a powerful force for social change.

Finally, it should be recognized that having someone as a friend is a form of power, which those without close friends do not have. It takes power to maintain friendships but communicative friends have it as their goal to move beyond power games to a situation where both voluntarily renounce power. Aristotle's perfect friend is simply an alter ego. With such friendship the Self is known to the Other more completely than in any other relationship, and this, of course, implies greater vulnerability. Such openness implies trust. Trust, a precondition of friendship, implies the absence of fear and with such trust there is also freedom to be truly oneself and do what one truly wants to do.

An anxious person is less likely to develop this open friendship, since Self, in a state of anxiety, is drawn in on itself in anxious self-examination. The overcoming of the negativity of the Self requires a vision of the good, which the Other must share. This need for value concurrence is crucial. Through such a shared vision of the good, friendship becomes a relationship which is essentially creative of the Self. This is why, in an age that is much obsessed with identity, true self and a sense of personal individuality, the development of pure, communicative friendship becomes a more generalized social, as well as personal, goal.

The fact that there are both private and public dimensions to friendship can make friendship dangerous to the wider society. Individuals make their commitment to each other without reference to group-derived status, norms and values and are likely to withhold information about the internal structure of their relationship in terms of its guiding norms and values from the outside world. Seen in these terms, as one observer put it, 'every friendship is thus a potential culture in miniature and also a potential counter-culture.'

Since one of the fundamental rules of friendship in all cultures is that gifts are given freely without thought of return, then friendship always tends towards equality between people. Friendships between people of widely diverse status, abilities or backgrounds are much less likely.

Friendship is a relationship built upon the whole person and aims at a psychological intimacy, which in this limited form makes it, in practice, a rare phenomenon, even though it may be more widely desired. It is a relationship based on freedom and is, at the same time, a guarantor of freedom. A society in which this kind of friendship is growing and flourishing is qualitatively different from a society based on the culturally reinforced norms of kinship and institutional roles and behaviour.

If I am correct in detecting this emerging aspect of contemporary social change, the consequences for our political system could be far-reaching. It could be the basis for a new style of social relationships. It is fundamentally egalitarian, individualistic and exclusive. In a sense, it is anti-political. It is a more mature social form than one based on dependence, superordination and subordination. It is subversive of market-based social relations: communicative friendship of character is based on generalized reciprocities. The introduction of quasi-accounting procedures undermines the very essence of communicative friendship. In contrast to the individualism of competitive market capitalism, where individual failure is an essential ingredient of the effectiveness of the system, individuality is about a distinctive style and identity and the unique capacity of everyone to be potentially lovable, not about hierarchies and effectiveness. Admittedly, this raises problems for those with difficulties in forming secure adult attachments. It implies that, in order for a citizen to be fully engaged in a good society, access to material resources is not enough: access to psychological resources is also necessary.

It is possible that progress in democracy will depend on a new generation that will increasingly locate itself in identity-shaping yet personally liberating, friendships. These sociable individuals who are striving to express themselves completely in friendships are, in a sense, deinstitutionalized. They do not see themselves primarily as housewife, trade unionist or manager. They are women and men who enjoy music, the countryside, the arts and who work to live, not live to work. A voluntary association such as the one for anglers may have more members than does the British Labour Party. How people live and who they are will be determined more by their friends than by their mothers or their superior line managers. We find out who we are as people with and through our friends. Friendship is about hope: between friends we talk about our futures, our ideals and larger-than-life meanings. There is an idealism in strong friendship because it is detached from the fixtures of role, status and custom. The deep communicating friendship of virtue described by Aristotle could be the basis for a vision of a society, which while probably impossible to achieve, provides a kind of active utopia that, in a sense, supersedes politics – certainly party politics – and from this point of view may be seen as dangerous by those at present in positions of power.

Conclusion

There is something about friendship that appears to be quintessentially post-modern. Overwhelmingly friendship has connotations of freedom, choice, individuality and, crucially, subversion. It is of the essence of friendship that it will escape the heavy-handed intrusions of social science. It is a form of what Philip Slater called 'social regression'. In some ways friendship has managed to escape while kinship, conjugal and sexual relations, attitudes to money and so much else have fallen to the objective scrutiny of sociologists, anthropologists and psychologists. Of course, this is not to say that we have not learnt much about friendship in the twentieth century. We see that it is heavily determined by the social structural circumstances of the time. By thinking about friendship we can understand something very important about the nature of the society in which it is embedded.

Every generation has to rethink friendship in its own terms. The social, economic, demographic and cultural changes at the end of the twentieth century emphasized choice, individualism and individuality. The various tensions and dialectics discussed in Chapter 3 above, resonate well. We seek both independence and dependence; we need choice, freedom and commitment and so on. Friendship can cope with these tensions better than the fixed and formal ties associated with family and organizations. Friendship has to be egalitarian and democratic: it has no place in hierarchies or authoritarian structures.

The social convoy that we associate with as we go through life – our fluctuating and ever-changing personal community – defines us, reflects us, supports us and so much else besides. It is most likely to include a partner, but it may not. It is also most likely to include close kin, but again it may not. We may not be able to understand the full depths of meaning associated with having a close, communicative friend until the last months of our life, or we may have known what it was when we were in our early twenties but have since lost that knowledge or understanding. Our lives may have both led us away from friends and brought them closer to us.

Most people's lives are too constrained and burdened to cope with the 'pure relationship' of friendship as defined by the philosophers. As Lynn Jamieson, in her admirably clear book *Intimacy*, put it, 'The ideal of the "pure relationship" does not allow for messy and asymmetrical periods of needing practical help or feeling dependent or needy which are routine occurrences in parent–child relationships, partnerships and some friendships. The circumstances of many people's lives render "pure" friendships both difficult and insufficient.' These may be comforting words for those who may be feeling 'friends-of-virtue-challenged' by some of the preceding discussion about the importance of that Aristotelian friendship form. It is clear that many men and women do manage to go through life perfectly well with 'good enough' relationships. They may never have experienced having a true, communicative friend, a soul-mate, a person who is like another self. Similarly, many people never have a life-long marriage or never have children. People who prefer or are obliged to live on their own are the most rapidly increasing household type. The woman who has a very wide circle of male friends but never settles with one may have chosen a lifestyle that causes grief to some of the men: but clearly that is her choice. She will know that she is more likely to live alone in her old age when her previous admirers have all gone to commit themselves to others. If she prefers to be solitary and have the space to live her life her way, that, surely, is a decision she has to make. She will recognize that this may involve loneliness from time to time, but some loneliness is part of the human condition. Those trapped all day with young children can feel so lonely that they become clinically depressed; others who are married to a kind, worthy, but basically dull and boring partner may feel acutely lonely at times.

I hope that readers will not pick up normative assumptions about the 'best' forms of friendship in this book that will make them feel inadequate in any way. Admittedly, the developmental psychologists and social policy engineers do come perilously close to fixing up pre-adolescents or elderly retired people with friendship packages designed to promote various outcomes that are perceived to be desirable. However, it would be just as outrageous to force everyone to be married on the grounds that happily married people are healthier and live longer as it would to foist friends on people. The man or woman who has the means and is more comfortable paying a housekeeper or a living-in nurse in their old age is entitled to do so. Those who know they will not be able to afford that in their old age and have no surviving kin may expect some support from public agencies, if their labour market position does not provide them with an adequate private pension. To make such people feel socially inadequate by giving them a low social-support rating is hardly very kind or humane.

There are many ways to live a life and the society that recognizes this and accepts a wide range of diversity is surely greatly to be desired.

A central theme of this book is that friends and friendship have to be seen in context. It would be equally misleading to talk in general terms about friendship based on information relating to eleventh century Western European monasteries as it would to generalize from case studies carried out in the gender divided United States of the 1970s. Women's and men's friendships are crucially affected by the social and material conditions in which they are grounded. So what is distinctive about Britain and America in the early years of the twenty-first century?

A number of familiar points need to be rehearsed. Women are by and large no longer totally economically dependent on male chief earners. This is partly because men's wages and salaries are in general insufficient to support a household and partly because many more women prefer to be in employment than be a dependant. Admittedly, many of the jobs that most women do are part-time, low paid and, in the case of such expanding areas as call centres, physically and emotionally draining. But women are moving into law, finance, banking and the medical professions in increasing numbers. In Britain women's full-time employment is increasing more rapidly than men's and is predicted to continue to do so.

Employment for both men and women is more flexible and is perceived to be more insecure, and the reduction of the importance of the psychological contract between employer and employee – that is, the exchange of security for loyalty – leads to a low-trust environment. As employees are encouraged to watch their own backs and be prepared to move on, they are less likely to trust and make friends with colleagues from work.

Not only is the employment context turbulent, insecure

and unpredictable, so also is the private sphere of family and household. If a work-wracked man could once return to the bosom of his family as a haven in the heartless world, he is now likely to return to an equally work-wracked partner and an exhausted child-minder or au pair.

In Britain workers with children have to fulfil their norms in child monitoring – homework checking, statutory reading aloud and such like – and those with older children may have the extra burden of their own elderly relatives to care for. Children may oppress and tyrannize their parents as they respond to television and peer pressure, insisting on the latest fashionable brand names for trainers, sports gear, leisure clothes and similar items which many parents can ill-afford. High levels of divorce, serial monogamy, early retirement and redundancy . . . the list is long and familiar. With all our national wealth – greater than at any time in the past – surveys do not prove that ordinary people are happier. Quite the contrary. Clinical depression has shown an unprecedented increase in the most advanced economies. Consumption increases but happiness does not follow. Survey after survey demonstrates a social polarization between the cash rich/time poor and the cash poor/time rich. The most frenetically active people in London, New York, Frankfurt or Milan may have great wealth but lack the time to enjoy it. Those with potentially the most choice have less time to exercise it.

Such people may claim to have lots of 'friends', and in a sense that might be true. Their address books are bulging. But friendship, as we have seen in this book, requires time and effort for it to flourish and flower. It requires time for talk and for intuitive understanding of the pauses and silences and a willingness to be open and vulnerable.

So what, precisely, are the prospects for friends and friendship in the context of late modernity? Friendship is the archetypal social relationship of choice, and ours is a period of choice – of clothes, style, fashion and identities – so, surely, friendship should be entering a golden age.

Certainly, with so much social turbulence there would seem to be a need for alternative sources of calmness and security in compensation. For many people this is supplied by their homes and gardens: home improvements – painting, decorating, extending, refurbishing – take up much time, as does gardening and the associated shopping. But all these activities require affirmation and approval from significant others. We want our chosen friends to admire our new kitchen or restyled garden. Ultimately we are social animals. The sociology of consumption must include a sociology of the audience of consumption.

So where do we find our friends and how do we maintain them? I consider that the expansion of higher education, especially among women, has greatly increased the capacity for making friends. A growing proportion of young people in their early twenties who are in higher or further education also have the time and opportunity to make friends to match their emerging identities. Later, when they have partners, children, ailing parents and all the hazards of getting through the life course, their friends could be there to support them. They may have experienced difficult divorces, cantankerous parents or problem children, but their common past holds them together. I have already commented on the importance of TV soap operas, such as *Friends*. Earlier soaps focused on family relationships – father–son or mother–daughter difficulties being central: now it is family–friend or friend–friend relations that bother people.

So how can friends be so central for those without the

time to nurture them? Modern technology in the form of telephone and e-mail helps: people can and do call each other late at night and e-mail each other regularly. One can take a cordless phone in the bath or hold it hunched on one's shoulder while cooking. People double up activities and inform each other what they are doing (Hi, it's me, I'm on the train).

As I wrote at the very beginning of this book, we are increasingly socially and culturally determined by our friends. This was not the case 100 years ago when one's family provided the central co-ordinates. Later, in mid-century, it was what the man in the household did to earn his living that placed his family in society. Now it is more the people we do things with that count. We are what our friends let us be: as skilled consumers we are adept at choosing our friends and they of choosing us. Yet underneath this apparently confident consumerism there is a deep unease, shown by the high incidence of mental disorders and depression. One answer to these problems of doubt, anxiety and the malaise of so-called risk society is to form good relationships. Perhaps a greater focus on friendship in the school curriculum during the early teenage years would be valuable. As I hope I have shown in this book, the topic is complex and challenging: I trust that I have done something to encourage readers to carry on exploring the ideals and practice of friends and friendship, both intellectually and in their personal lives.

Further Reading

The subject of friendship has been approached through literature, philosophy, politics, psychology, sociology and anthropology, but the general reader interested in the topic would do well
to keep clear of student texts. A delightful way to start would be
through *The Oxford Book of Friendship*, edited by D. J. Enright
and David Rawlinson (Oxford University Press, 1991). For
those who want an accessible and most useful compendium of
the classical texts on friendship, the anthology edited by Michael
Pakaluk *Other Selves: Philosophers on Friendship* (Hackett, 1991)
is indispensable. A book that brings together psychoanalysis,
philosophy and sociology with dazzling panache and which is
brimming with ideas (and controversy) is Graham Little's
Friendship: Being Ourselves with Others (Melbourne: Text, 1993),
but it is hard to find (the ISBN is 1-86372 024-3). Little has an
essay in *The Dialectics of Friendship*, edited by Roy Porter and
Sylvana Tomaselli (Routledge, 1989), and the references in that
collection extend well beyond the social sciences. For a quirky
account by an anthropologist, Robert Brain's *Friends and Lovers*
(Hart-Davis MacGibbon, 1976) would encourage the general
reader to explore the nature of friendship more comparatively
and cross-culturally. Sociologists have a distinctive vocabulary
that may deter those from different traditions. Some of the
essays by Georg Simmel are particularly rewarding and full of
insight. See *The Sociology of Georg Simmel*, edited by Kurt H.
Wolff (Free Press of Glencoe, 1950). For a more recent general
introduction Anthony Giddens's *The Transformation of Intimacy:*

Sexuality, Love and Eroticism in Modern Societies (Polity Press, 1992) sets an agenda that many have since followed.

Students' texts

There are a number of introductory texts to the sociology of friendship, and the interested reader who follows up references will soon be able to gain a systematic grasp of the field. Lynn Jamieson's *Intimacy: Personal Relationships in Modern Society* (Polity Press, 1998) is an authoritative overview, putting friendship in the context of family and couple relationships very convincingly. Other good introductory texts for British students are Graham Allan's *Friendship: Developing a Sociological Perspective* (Harvester Wheatsheaf, 1989) and *Kinship and Friendship in Modern Britain* (Oxford University Press, 1996). For those more familiar with the basic student literature, a recent collection of original essays, edited by Rebecca G. Adams and Graham Allan, *Placing Friendship in Context* (Cambridge University Press, 1998), explores some of the research frontiers of the subject.

Recent texts published in the United States include Beverley Fehr's *Friendship Processes* (Sage, 1996) and Rosemary Blieszner and Rebecca G. Adams's *Adult Friendships* (Sage, 1992). While these are thorough and competent canters through the literature, I do not recommend them for the general reader. William K. Rawlins's *Friendship Matters: Communication Dialectics and the Life Course* (Aldine de Gruyter, 1992) is clearly and imaginatively written. I draw on this book in Chapter 3, which I hope will encourage readers to go back to the original.

More Detailed References

Introduction

I do not intend to provide detailed references to all the books and authors I mention. That would be an unnecessary burden on a short book of this nature. However, it may be helpful to provide some signposts to my journey through often quite extensive literatures.

In the Introduction I mention the notion of social capital. The debate seems to have been sparked off by Robert D. Putnam in his study of civic life in Italy *Making Democracy Work* (Princeton University Press, 1993), but recent academic discussion on both sides of the Atlantic tends to adopt a wary, if not sceptical, stance. Two key papers are Alejandro Portes's 'Social Capital: Its Origins and Applications in Modern Sociology' (*Annual Review of Sociology*, 24 (1998), 1–24) and Peter A. Hall's 'Social Capital in Britain' (*British Journal of Political Science*, 29 (1999), 417–61).

The study of social networks has generated a large and sometimes overcomplex literature. I personally believe it is best to start with the social anthropologists, who, typically, keep their feet on the ground. J. Clyde Mitchell's edited collection *Social Networks in Urban Situations* (published for the Institute for Social Research at the University of Zambia by Manchester University Press, 1969) is a classic collection still of great value. Another landmark study is Claude S. Fischer's *To Dwell Among Friends: Personal Networks in Town and City* (University of Chicago Press, 1982).

Chapter 1   What is Friendship?

As a non-specialist, I found Suzanne Stern-Gillet's text *Aristotle's Philosophy of Friendship* (State University of New York Press, 1995) much the clearest exposition of that topic. However, Horst Hutter's *Politics as Friendship: The Origins of Classical Notions of Politics in the Theory and Practice of Friendship* (Wilfrid Laurier University Press, 1978) is also very helpful. Those who want to pursue this area in depth will find the bibliography of David Konstan's *Friendship in the Classical World* (Cambridge University Press, 1997) very useful, although the text itself is disappointing.

A very full source for the exploration of medieval Christian friendship is *Friendship and Community: The Monastic Experience 350–1250*, by Brian Patrick McGuire (Kalamazoo, MI: Cistercian Studies Series no. 95, Cistercian Publications Inc., 1988).

For an astringent discussion of clientage and instrumental friendship by an anthropologist, see the chapter on politics by John Davis in *People of the Mediterranean* (Routledge & Kegan Paul, 1977). The references cited therein will direct readers to the more detailed community studies in Greece and Spain to which I refer.

Chapter 2   Friendship, Modernity and Trust

Two fine articles by Allan Silver influenced me heavily in the writing of this chapter. These are 'Friendship in Commercial Society: Eighteenth Century Social Theory and Modern Sociology' (*American Journal of Sociology*, 95 (1990), 1474–504) and 'Friendship and Trust as Moral Ideals: An Historical Approach' (*European Journal of Sociology*, 30 (1989), 274–97). The study by Peter Willmott, also referred to in the previous chapter, is *Friendship Networks and Social Support* (Policy Studies Institute, 1987).

Chapter 3   Friendship and the Self

The most important references in this chapter have already been referred to above. The chapter by Harrison appears in the volume edited by Adams and Allan. Another useful source is *Exchange and Power in Social Life* by Peter M. Blau (John Wiley & Sons, 1964), and the argument has bearing on many of the themes discussed in this book.

Chapter 4   Friendship in Context

The literature of developmental psychology is dauntingly large. However, three important collections cover a wide span of issues and, with these as starting points, there should be no difficulty in following up specific issues in the relevant specialist journals. These are *The Development of Children's Friendships* edited by Steven R. Asher and John M. Gottman (Cambridge University Press, 1981), *Conversations of Friends: Speculations on Affective Development* edited by John M. Gottman and Jeffrey G. Parker (Cambridge University Press, 1986) – especially Chapter 1, 'The Importance of Friendship' – and *The Company They Keep: Friendship in Childhood and Adolescence*, edited by William M. Bukowski, Andrew F. Newcomb and Willard W. Hartup (Cambridge University Press, 1996). A very important chapter in this last collection, by Thomas J. Berndt, 'Exploring the Effects of Friendship Quality on Social Development', was one I draw on quite heavily. The other article to which I refer in more detail is 'Preadolescent Friendship and Peer Rejection as Predictors of Adult Adjustment', by Catherine L. Bagwell, Andrew F. Newcomb and William M. Bukowski, in *Child Development*, 69 (1998), 140–53.

Women's friendships have also generated a large literature. *Best Friends and Marriage* by Stacey J. Oliker (University of California Press, 1989) is an interesting case study of a particular social category in a particular context. Pat O'Connor's text

Friendships Between Women: A Critical Review (Harvester Wheat-sheaf, 1992) covers the literature very thoroughly. Dorothy Jerrome has published a number of useful articles on elderly women's friendship – see, for example, 'The Significance of Friendship for Women in Later Life', in *Ageing and Society*, 1 (1981), 175–97, and her monograph *Good Company* (Edinburgh University Press, 1992), especially Chapter 5 on friendship.

Graham Allan's essay 'Friendship and the Private Sphere' appears in the collection *Placing Friendship in Context*, mentioned above. Another very useful essay, by B. Bradford Brown, is 'A Life-Span Approach to Friendship: Age-Related Dimensions of an Ageless Relationship', in *Research in the Interweave of Social Roles*, 2 (1981), 22–50.

The work of Sarah Matthews is among the best ethnography on friendship. See *Friendships Through the Life Course: Oral Biographies in Old Age* (Sage, 1986) and her chapter in *Later Life: The Social Psychology of Ageing*, edited by Victor W. Marshall (Sage, 1986).

Perhaps the most seminal essay for the theoretical understanding of friendship over the life-course is that by Robert L. Kahn and Toni C. Antonucci, 'Convoys Over the Life Course: Attachment, Roles and Social Support', in *Life-Span Development and Behaviour*, vol. 3 (Academic Press, 1980). More recently published is Toni C. Antonucci and Hiroko Akiyama's 'Convoys of Social Relations: Family and Friendships Within a Life-Span Context', in *Handbook of Ageing and the Family*, edited by Rosemary Blieszner and Victoria H. Bedford (Greenwood Press, 1995).

Chapter 5 Social Capital and the Politics of Friendship

There is a very rapidly developing literature on social support, partly because of its direct relevance for psychoneuroimmunology. Perhaps the best place to start would be the collection edited by Barbara R. Sarason et al. called *Social Support: An*

Interactional View (John Wiley & Sons, 1990). A very thorough review of recent literature, 'The Relationship Between Social Support and Psychological Processes: A Review with Emphasis on Underlying Mechanisms and Implications for Health', by Bert N. Uchino et al., appears in the *Psychological Bulletin* 119 (1996), 488–531.

References on social capital were referred to in the section on the Introduction. Vladimir Shlapentokh's book *The Public and Private Life of the Soviet People* was published by Oxford University Press in 1989.

The relationship between social networks and finding employment is put forward by M. Granovetter in *Getting a Job: A Study of Contacts and Careers* (Harvard University Press, 1974) and is given rigorous statistical corroboration by Carmel Hannan in *Social Cohesion and Unemployment Exit Rates* (Institute for Labour Research and Institute for Social and Economic Research, University of Essex, 1998).

Conclusion

Some of my argument in the final paragraphs has been influenced by a stimulating paper by Robert E. Lane, 'The Road Not Taken: Friendship, Consumerism and Happiness', in *Critical Review* (Fall 1994).

I recognize that many may feel that the essence of friendship may be lost through the burning focus of rigorous empirical research. Unquestionably some of the greatest insights into its nature have been achieved by novelists and biographers. I hope that, by being alerted to some of the problems and issues associated with friends and friendship, readers may be encouraged to deepen their understanding through their general reading of novels from Jane Austen to Virginia Woolf – and on to Tim Lott!

Index

Lightning Source UK Ltd.
Milton Keynes UK
177605UK00001B/19/P